DARK TRANSFERENCE

The Sequel to Estate of Horror

Anita Jo Intenzo

This is a true story. Some of the names of places, groups and people, and of Paul's family and friends, have been changed for privacy reasons. It is not my intention to embarrass or defame anyone but to present the facts just as I discovered them. It is up to the reader to draw their own conclusions as to what they believe.

ISBN-10:0692770569
ISBN-13:9780692770566

DEDICATION

For my cousin Ellen Masci and friend Ann Marie Pelosi,
who believed in me about my haunting experiences.
They left us too soon but will always be in our hearts.

ACKNOWLEDGEMENTS

It's not easy having me for a client. It is not every day that someone comes to you with a manuscript about a truly scary paranormal experience and you decide to take them on. Only then you realize what you got yourself into. That brave person is my agent Laurie Hawkins. Over four years ago she read my manuscript for *Estate of Horror,* the work of a first-time author, and took a chance on me. Her hunch that my story would be read by many others paid off. In fact, my story became an episode for a national TV show. Not bad!

There have been "bumps in the night" along the way. Laurie has experienced some very strange occurrences at her home office while printing out my manuscript for *Estate of Horror* and now my sequel *Dark Transference.* She had ghostly experiences before she met me but things have only escalated. There has been poltergeist activity and sightings of a little girl at her home. Things have disappeared and then turned up in the strangest places. Computer files have evaporated on her desk-top and her printer has been known to spit out parts across the room!

We have found we have been deliberately thwarted in getting this second book out. It has been difficult for me to properly juxtaposition the last six years of the many supernatural incidents and to combine them in a coherent story compared to *Estate of Horror's* time frame of only ten months. That is why there has been the delay in getting the sequel published. Citing these factors, it has not been an easy project for either Laurie or me. We both have dealt with serious personal health issues with parents over these last four years, too. I can only thank Laurie from the bottom of my heart that she has stuck with me through every weird thing. She has faithfully edited me through each chapter to help me put together a book we are both proud of. I hope you readers will think so too.

I want to thank my son Chris for writing the Foreword to this book. Without his constant support I could not do any of this. He has born the gift of his reawakened psychic abilities with humor and grace. He is an immensely talented person and I know he will go far with his new miniature hobby store, Enter the Realm. Love you son!

To my loving parents who did not live to see my first book published and watch their daughter and grandson on national TV. They would be over the moon! To the rest of my family and friends who have stuck by me through this paranormal journey even though they have a hard time understanding just exactly what we are dealing with, I am grateful beyond words.

Next I'd like to thank Laurie Hull (McCabe) for her time and tremendous gifts as a psychic medium, along with members of her investigative team that came to my house, at times under dangerous and stressful conditions. Sorry about the camera, Mark.

To the production crew who made my book trailer for *Estate of Horror*: Ken McVey at MRS Audio Visual, Joe Lavin, and Bill Hilferty and Jack Nitz of JBT Productions. Thank you for making it such a unique and successful trailer and for inadvertently capturing our Shadow Man on video. Joe Lavin is involved in making independent films, and Bill and Jack are now living in Los Angeles and premiered their first film, *The Bad Kids*, at the Sundance Movie Festival in February 2016. All success to all of you!

Lastly, I want to thank Bill Bean, who has not only become a dear friend but family. His love and sincere help to us as a divine deliverance minister has been a gift from God. Given his high stature in the paranormal community, Bill's endorsement of our horrific paranormal experiences has lent an air of credibility that is priceless and something we will never forget.

My heart is full of gratitude to so many others not mentioned. You know who you are. I know this life is only a precursor to the next. There is a joyful journey that awaits us all!

TABLE OF CONTENTS

FOREWORD

I like to call my mom a Renaissance woman and I am not exaggerating when I say that or because she is my mom. I often take for granted her many gifts and talents as an artist, teacher, graphic designer, entrepreneur, business owner, lecturer and now author. Her motto is to *Live Art!*

She is also one of the smartest people I know. You could ask her anything about history, especially ancient Egypt, and she would be able to tell you more than you ever needed to know. My grandmother always called her, "a walking encyclopedia." She has always been a prolific reader and has instilled in me a love of art, books and the written word. It is her many interests that led her to Paul Jaeger and a friendship based on mutual respect for each other's professions. He was also one of the kindest and smartest people I ever met. No wonder my mom and Paul shared a long thirty-year friendship. Paul trusted my mom to be his executor because he knew what a loyal and honest person she was.

That is why it came as a great shock to me after Paul died that we encountered the hauntings at his house. Paul was such a nice guy and I couldn't figure out why we were being targeted in such a manner. As we spent months cleaning out his house, I have never been so emotionally involved with such negative energy that affected me both physically and mentally. I was so afraid for my mom to be there alone that I could not abandon her even though being at the house made me physically ill.

Did I mention ghosts? Yes there were ghosts! I know many do not believe in such things but we had many friends who were non-believers and witnessed unexplainable things that changed them forever. They still to this day talk about the things flying around the room, the smell of a wet cat, the scratching noises in the walls, shadowy figures and disembodied voices telling us to GET OUT!

I'm so proud of my mom that she never wavered from the difficult challenge of being Paul's executor no matter how unpleasant and terrifying things got. That is why I was happy that she had decided to write her first book, *Estate of Horror* and now this sequel, *Dark Transference.* She has once again gathered her courage to tell the story of the dark trespassers that have now taken up residence in our house. Writing has been a cathartic exercise for her over the last seven years. Her mission is to let others know that they are not alone in the "Paranormal Club" and that supernatural things can occur when least expected, even when it begins with an innocent friendship.

My mom and I have been on a long journey together to find out the truth of why this happened to us. We have been on a quest for answers and hopefully readers will understand how difficult it has been for us to make sense of all this. The haunting dreams I've experienced that are documented here are 100% real. My mom and I live a paranormal life every day. As our good friend Bill Bean says, "We do not seek these things out, they seek us." We are still not sure if we have fully explained why we were sought by these dark entities but we choose to live in the light always.

- Chris Levis

INTRODUCTION

Seven years ago, on a cold and snowy day in January, 2009, I stood in front of a group of mourners in a church to give the eulogy for my deceased friend, Paul Jaeger. Paul and I were close friends for over thirty years, throughout which we had shared our love of art, anthropology, history and more. What he didn't share with me, however, were dark, family secrets that would be revealed to me as I fulfilled the responsibility as executor to clean out and sell his home.

The nine months my son Chris and I spent in the house have forever changed our lives, and what we experienced there became the subject of my debut book, *Estate of Horror, A True Story of Haunting, Hatred and a Horrific Family Secret.* Standing before the friends assembled at Paul's memorial service, I couldn't have imagined that I would now be an author, having fulfilled the promise to myself to tell my story of the incredible haunting and poltergeist experience we survived at the small, 3-bedroom house that my friend had called home.

It was important to me to share my story publicly. My story is true but I've had to defend myself to skeptics who questioned that it was my imagination and that I made it all up. Believe me; I do not have that wild an imagination! It has been suggested by some skeptics that Chris faked the poltergeist activity presented on our videos on YouTube. Let me just say poltergeist activity is a very rare event. You would never believe that statement to be true with all the rampant "supernatural activity" that happens on today's paranormal TV shows. I am not saying things don't happen on those shows but remember these are primary entertainment venues and they have to give the audience something "creepy" so they will tune in next week. When we recorded our paranormal events we did it for our own documentation at the time, never thinking they would later be reference in a book and then on a TV show, *A Haunting*. That was the furthest thing on our minds. We were more interested in surviving.

So many people have had similar experiences like mine but they fear telling others because of the possible ridicule and disbelief. I wrote *Estate of Horror* for them, for the people who are not able or willing to write about their supernatural encounters and the heartbreak that they have suffered alone by keeping silent. I feel your pain.

I had never intended that I would be writing a sequel. I simply wanted to tell my incredible and true ghost story and be done with it. Unfortunately, that was wishful thinking.

I.

They're Here!

December 2009-May 2010

"There is no death. There is only a transition to a different sphere of consciousness."

-TANGINA-Poltergeist, the movie 1984

CHAPTER 1
OUT OF THIN AIR

"Good morning, Mom. Can you believe it's Christmas Eve?"

"I know. You want some waffles and bacon?"

"That sounds good. What time are we going over to Nana and Poppy's?"

"I told Rose to be at your grandparents by five and ..."

PING!

"Did you hear that?"

"Hear what? Come on Chris; put the maple syrup on the table."

"I don't know. I think I'm hearing things."

"So, I still have to pick up the crab cakes and some cans of minced clams for the pasta. We should be over there no later than ..."

BANG!

Chris and I froze in our tracks. What was going on? Those sounds were inside the house and we were the only ones there. We looked at each other across my dining room table and knew only too well that familiar sound. My heart beat faster; I was afraid. I didn't know if I could handle another nine months like those that had just passed. I thought that when we cleaned out and sold Paul's house after he passed away that we would be done with all of the paranormal. No more things thrown around the room; no strange voices that came from nowhere. No more ghostly shadows creeping across the floor and no one being pushed or scratched.

We knew we still needed answers to some things left unsolved. There was the question of Paul's father's past and the real origin of one of Paul's bequeathed items. But now, the sound I heard told me that it might not be over.

Chris and I left the dining room and made a beeline down the hallway, convinced that is where we heard the bang. A small plastic mat cutter lay near the front door of the house. Lying on the rug next to it was a woman's tortoise shell hairclip. We recognized the small black retractable mat cutter as something we kept in the kitchen, on top of our microwave, to open small packages, but we did not recognize the hairclip.

"What's going on, Mom?"

"I don't know. This hair clip isn't mine. It's as if it materialized out of thin air. Maybe it's something we packed at Paul's house and brought here, but I can't be sure."

We spent several minutes looking around for other objects and found nothing. We were back in familiar territory. It seemed to be the kind of poltergeist activity that Chris and I, and many friends and colleagues, had experienced at Paul's.

I called out to the spirits as I looked all around the foyer and hallway. "If you are going to throw stuff, I wish it wasn't junk. How about sending us a twenty-dollar gold piece?"

"That would be a nice Christmas present!"

"Please, let's have breakfast before anything else happens." I headed for the kitchen, feeling shaky.

All had been quiet since Paul's house was no longer our responsibility and we turned it over to the new buyers in October of 2009. But we weren't completely surprised at this new activity. Our psychic friend, Laurie Hull of Tri-County Paranormal, the paranormal investigating group that I had called for help as we faced the ghosts at Paul's, had warned us. She and her group had been instrumental in finding answers for us there, even helping Paul to come through her medium, Randy, to communicate with us. But Laurie was fearful that we had brought home several spirits which were attached to artifacts that Paul had left me and which were now stored in our basement. She said there were no guarantees or an exact science when dealing with the spirit realm.

But it was now Christmas, several months since then, and it seemed like our attempts to get back to living a more normal existence were working out. Chris and I were trying to catch up with our Christmas shopping and take care of all of the many errands that the holiday requires. I started making plans for a wonderful get-together with my friend Rose on Christmas Eve at my parent's house. This would be Rose's first Christmas without her mother, so it had to be special.

The activity stopped as suddenly as it came and we busied ourselves getting ready for the evening. Chris and I were upstairs in his bedroom discussing what Christmas presents we had to take to my parents' house when suddenly, something solid hit against the ceramic tile in the bathroom. I ducked when I heard the loud noise.

"WHOA!"

I went into the bathroom and spied a shiny yellow-colored coin on the floor. It couldn't be! Did the ghosts hear my wish and answer us with a real gold coin? I picked it up and saw what appeared to be a very old car wash token. I had never seen one like it before. I saw that it had an area code that was no longer used in our county, and inscribed on it was the name of the town where the Jaegers – Paul's family - had lived before moving to the house that I had spent almost a year cleaning out. Where it came from, I had no idea.

"Hmmm, jokes on us, Mom," Chris started to laugh, "but it *is* gold… sort of."

"Thanks a lot," I called out to the unseen spirits, "Again, another piece of worthless junk. You can do better than that!"

We stepped out into the hallway and something else hit the same ceramic tiled wall, but harder.

"Oh my God, Mom, look!"

On the floor shone a bright, shiny Morgan silver dollar.

A sickening realization entered my mind as I saw the date on the silver dollar of 1914 and remembered, from going through all the family's papers and the death certificate, that Paul's father was born that year.

"Do you think they came from Paul's house?" Chris asked.

"Please, don't even say it out loud," I cautioned as I sat down on my bed facing the hallway. I needed to collect my thoughts.

"I'm going to take a shower, Mom. Try to relax."

Chris had walked into the bathroom and started to shut the door, when suddenly I saw a tall black shadow dart along the ceiling towards the bathroom and follow him inside.

"Chris! Look out!"

The door flew open and his electric shaver and attachments flew out of the bathroom as if they were thrown with amazing force. I watched as they smashed against the opposite wall.

"Son-of-a-bitch!" yelled Chris. "Look what they did!"

"Is it broken?" I asked, kneeling down on the floor beside him to help pick up the pieces. As I looked down to the first floor, I saw the image of a black shadow race along the stairs to the bottom of the steps. It seemed to break up into smaller balls of shadows that quickly flew to the left of the hallway. A cold chill ran up my spine.

"No! This cannot be! Not here!" I was screaming, near tears. This could not be happening all over again. Not in my house! Frantic, I called out to the first person that came to my mind.

"Please Paul, help me. It's Christmas Eve! Tell them to stop. I want peace!"

Anger took over for fear. I couldn't even have the relaxing holiday I felt I so richly deserved.

Suddenly, there was silence. Miraculously, the activity stopped. This wasn't the first time that Paul had helped me from the beyond. Now that it appeared that our house was just what Paul Jaeger's house once was – very haunted – I would need him even more.

CHAPTER 2
GHOSTS OF CHRISTMAS

Christmas Eve dinner at my parent's house with Rose was quiet but a bit unsettling as we discussed the disturbing events from earlier that afternoon.

"I thought this was all taken care of," my mother said.

She was concerned now, as she had been during all the time Chris and I were working at Paul's house. We always assured her we would be safe, but she was a mother and she still worried.

More important, though, was the fact that I was concerned for her and my father, as both were elderly and had been experiencing serious health problems for some time. If all of the paranormal activity was difficult for Chris and I, it was doubly so for them.

"At Paul's house maybe, Nana," answered Chris, "but we were warned that we could have activity at our house. Things have been quiet since we sold the house and I thought for sure we were going to be okay."

"You forget, Chris," I reminded him, "we have been rummaging in the basement the past few weeks, organizing boxes and looking for that alien ... whatever you call it ... artifact, so maybe it unsettled them."

Those words took me back to Paul's house the night of October 13th, 2009 when Chris and I first met Laurie Hull and her team from Tri-County paranormal, which included Clare and her husband Randy, a psychic medium.

We all settled ourselves in the living room while Randy took a side chair near a table where I had set up an 8" x 10" framed picture of Paul in his best "Indiana Jones" hat, smiling in front of some South American Indian ruins. For several minutes, there was complete silence. Then, I heard heavy breathing coming from Randy. His eyes were closed and he seemed to be going into a trance.

"Paul, please talk to us. We can help you if you're having problems being here."

Only Randy's very heavy, deep breathing broke the silence. Another minute went by and then Randy spoke, but I knew it was Paul.

"Why are you here?"

"I'm very upset with myself."

"We don't want you to be upset. Who is speaking?" Laurie asked.

"My name is Paul."

"Anita and Chris have asked us to be here. We want to help. We are sorry your life was cut short. We want to know why you haven't moved into the light."

"Can't. I'm very upset."

"Is there a reason why you're upset and haven't moved on...into the light?" Laurie asked.

"Unfinished business. There's an artifact...that you took home...that's not of this world."

"Paul, can you describe it to Anita?" Clare asked.

"Ummm...cough...it is like stone. It's similar to pottery, but...more like marble."

"Do you want Anita and Chris to find it?"

"The artifact is in the wrong hands. They shouldn't have it…not good for them."

"I have no idea what he's talking about," Chris said.

"Maybe I can draw it for you," Laurie suddenly volunteered. "I'm getting a picture of something. Do you guys have a piece of paper and pen?"

At that moment, a deep, unfamiliar voice was recorded on Chris' digital recorder shouting a command,. "Don't draw it!"

We waited as she drew the object. Randy still had his eyes closed and was still in a trance.

She showed the drawing to Chris and me but we didn't recognize the object at all.

"This is what I came up with. It's small with a slender body and a bulbous head with writing or designs on it. I don't know. Do you remember seeing anything like this in the house?"

"I don't remember seeing anything like that," I said. "Is there some kind of other world demon or evil spirit attached to one of the objects, Laurie?"

"It's something else."

"What do you want Anita and Chris to do?" Laurie asked Paul.

"It has to be buried. I didn't prepare myself." Paul sounded annoyed with himself.

"I think they're confused," Clare said.

"It should have been buried with me."

I told Laurie and Clare that Paul had not been buried but had been cremated and his ashes spread out over a mountaintop in Colorado.

"Do you want Anita and Chris to bury it someplace now?" Clare asked.

"It should not fall into the wrong hands. It won't be good for them."

"If Anita and Chris find this object, where do you want them to bury it?"

"It should be put back where I got it."

Silence fell over the room.

"Ok. Where did you get it?" Laurie asked.

"Peru."

Laurie broke in with her impression and a possible explanation of what Paul had just said.

"I think what I'm getting is that it was dug up from a grave site. A farmer on his land found it and he sold it to Paul. It was like, here's a rich American looking for artifacts and he's got the money to buy it, and he sold it to him. I don't think he really knew what he had in his possession. He had no idea what it was."

"Can you describe it to us as best you can?" Laurie asked more insistently.

"It has the ability to change shape…at will. It is not a good thing to have in the house." There was urgency in his voice.

"That doesn't sound like anything Native American to me," I said.

"It was not of this world," Paul insisted.

"What is it then? Is it some kind of meteorite or something?" Chris asked.

"No, I think it's an alien artifact, guys," Laurie stated. She was dead serious.

Randy's message from Paul about the artifact that he purchased in Peru, which Paul called dangerous and described as "not of this world," ran through my head. Could this item, which we had not yet found or identified, really be as lethal as Paul had said?

"Tell them to unsettle this!" Chris exclaimed as he extended a middle finger in the air.

"Umm, I don't think that will help, Chris," Rose spoke up. "It's your house Anita; those spirits don't have a right to be there. You should keep alert for any more of the activity and if it gets worse, I would call that paranormal investigative team that helped you to cross Paul over to the other side. You trusted them before, now it's time for them to come to *your* house and see what they can find and help you out."

"The sooner the better," my Mom chimed in. "Now, who wants a piece of my chocolate cream yule log?" My mother was the master of changing the subject in mid-sentence.

We didn't need to be asked twice as we all delved into the delicious dessert.

As I ate a piece of the cake, I thought of how many others in my community were having a very normal holiday dinner, anticipating the gift giving tomorrow and the chance to have a peaceful time with loved ones on such a festive holiday. I envied them, yet despite what had happened earlier, I had much to be grateful for, as I had just lived through one of the most traumatic times in my life that affected me both physically and mentally.

In fulfilling the demanding task of disposing of my friend's estate, I learned of my strong willpower and capability for enduring a highly emotional and dangerously charged atmosphere. We had confronted the realms of the supernatural and survived. I had a few physical scars that would eventually go away but the emotional scars would be lingering much longer. Was I kidding myself? I had been in denial by using humor and laughter in response to just how dark and dangerous the horrors at Paul's house were. I realized now that it wasn't over and wondered if it ever would be. I was angry, but also sad. In this season of celebrating the Savior's birth, who forgave his tormentors and ultimately his killers, could I also forgive my friend with his many secrets? These devastating secrets seemed to reach from beyond the grave and continue to haunt us. What they had done to me and my family was irreversible. Could I forgive, considering the circumstances now?

I went to bed that night, but could not sleep. Instead of sugarplums dancing in my head, images of the paranormal activity we had experienced only a few short hours before replayed endlessly. I felt like my son and I were entering an entirely new chapter of the unknown, which we had not anticipated. I wanted it to be finished. The supernatural stuff was supposed to stop when we closed the door on Paul's house and settled the estate. Whatever dark transference had carried over to my house, it looked like we would now have to confront it. We had no idea what we were dealing with.

My once loving home, where I raised my son as a single parent, had always been my refuge and source of pride and accomplishment. There was a lot of blood, sweat, and tears I shed trying to keep it going for years to make a home for my son and me. Was it now destined to become a battleground for possession between the seemingly malicious dark supernatural entities and us? I had to face the facts. I might now be living a *paranormal life.* I sat up in bed and made a vow. This was my home and I would be damned if I was going to let them win! I was not afraid - I was mad!

CHAPTER 3
GROUND ZERO

Early one afternoon in January, Chris was cleaning in his bedroom - a New Year's resolution he made to himself. We'd made it through the holidays without further incident, which was a relief, and we had reached a new year. 2010 was the time to start on making all the changes we promised ourselves.

Chris had always been a movie buff and his vast collection of entertainment items reflected that. Besides his action figures, he had thousands of Warhammer miniature models that he had expertly painted. His room contained posters, magazines, hundreds of DVD's, CD's and other assorted movie memorabilia. As he worked, he started to notice that things kept disappearing and then reappearing in another area of his room.

CLANG! BANG!

"What the...? I guess they don't like that I'm cleaning my room," Chris said aloud.

"What's going on?" I asked, but I had an idea that the poltergeist activity was starting again. Chris was still on the second floor as I began picking up coins and a keychain in the downstairs hallway.

"They just threw that stuff down there," Chris explained to me as I walked up the stairs.

I found him sitting in the hallway outside his bedroom with the piles of magazines surrounding him when he frantically started searching around him.

"They were right HERE!" His fist pounded the floor.

"What?"

"Where's my pile of *White Dwarf* magazines? They're gone! They were right next to me and now they're suddenly gone!"

"They have to be around here somewhere. A big pile of magazines doesn't just suddenly disappear."

I should have known better. I was standing in the hallway near my bedroom door when a CD case flew from Chris' room and hit the doorframe next to me.

"Hey!" Chris yelled. "Stop throwing my shit around. If you want do that, go back to the other house and play with the construction workers, you undead assholes!"

PLOP!

I turned around and saw the pile of the missing magazines just plop down on the floor, right in front of me, as they dropped right out of thin air. I jumped back!

"What the hell!" Chris shouted. "Did you see that?"

A dime then flew right past me, into my bedroom. I let out a nervous laugh -- these ghosts were big spenders!

"Yeah, real funny, wait till *your* things get thrown," Chris warned.

Chris finished up in his room as quickly as possible.

The activity died down. But a far more troubling scenario loomed on the horizon. We didn't know it yet but what would come would once again unsettle us to the core.

⁂

A little over a week later, on January 10, Chris and I had arrived home from my parent's house around 7:00 in the evening and were settling in for a very chilly night. Chris was upstairs taking a bath and I talked on the phone to a friend for about twenty minutes. At 8:45 p.m., the power blinked. Once, twice, then it blinked again. Suddenly, I was blind as I was plunged into total darkness.

As I stood in the doorway of my first-floor art studio still holding the phone, suddenly something hit me on the right shoulder. My poor friend didn't know what was happening as she heard my startled scream on the other end.

"What's going on over there Anita? Maybe you should call the police!"

I quickly explained that it wasn't an intruder, at least not in the physical sense. I told her I'd call her back and quickly hung up the phone.

"Chris!" I yelled to him upstairs. "I just got hit."

"What? What's going on?" he yelled back from the bathroom. Chris ran downstairs like lightning, wrapped in his bath towel, holding his cell phone. It was a comical sight in the midst of the confusion.

"What the hell, Mom?"

"Look there!" I pointed to the floor as he used his phone's light to illuminate the area. It was a black plastic spear, with a Guinness Beer label on it.

"That's the kind of thing you put on a steak in a restaurant. Where the hell did that come from?" Chris asked me. He was shaking like a leaf.

"How the hell would I know?"

Something else made a noise as it was thrown in the studio. Then I heard the plastic box of a music cassette tape smash on the tile floor as it flew into the studio's bathroom.

"Jesus!" I stood motionless, afraid to turn around. I said a silent prayer.

I looked out my studio window and saw that the streetlights on the other side of the street and up the block were still on. Only our house was dark. More cassette tapes flew into the bathroom and the sounds of metal coins hit the front door. It was unnerving and terrifying to be suddenly plunged into darkness and then hearing objects coming out of nowhere and thrown around you.

We were now at the mercy and totally under the control of something unknown.

"Come upstairs with me," Chris told me. "I don't want you to get hurt!"

"Yeah, I will in a minute."

My first instinct was to quickly call my parents who only lived a few blocks away. I wondered if their lights were out. They were concerned about our situation. My mom could hear how upset I was and said to come to their house as soon as we could. I realized then our cars were stuck in the garage with the electric door opener, useless without power. I told them we would be okay and I would call them later. As I hung up the phone, another object flew into the studio.

This was getting out of hand!

Chris decided he'd better go upstairs and get dressed and as he headed for the stairs, there were loud bangs coming from the front door of the house. The door was right outside my studio, so easily reached. We both looked at each other not knowing what to do next.

"Should I open the door?" I whispered to him.

"NO! What is wrong with you? I'll be right down … two seconds."

"Well, what should I do?"

I stood frozen at the doorway and I could feel myself starting to panic.

"Ask who it is if they knock again," Chris yelled from upstairs.

Then I heard it: several light rapid taps, like coming from a child's desperate hand, sounded from the front door. These didn't sound threatening. Was it a neighbor? Did someone need our help?

"Hello?" I shouted as I stepped cautiously toward it. There was no answer. There is an admonition about hearing a knock on the front door of your house and finding no one knocking. Against better judgment, I opened the door, bracing myself for whatever I was going to confront. No one was there. Only a cold, still darkness stood in front of me.

I quickly closed the door and as I did, a brown plastic doorstop from the upstairs bathroom hit it, just missing me.

"Hurry up Chris!"

Chris, now dressed, bolted down the steps in seconds with his cell phone once again the only light source we had.

"Why did you open the door? You *never* open the door!" stated Chris.

"It sounded like a child that needed help."

"Maybe, that's what *they* want you to think."

He had a good point.

We quickly walked through the downstairs hall toward the back of the house and away from the door, to get to our emergency stash of candles and flashlights in the kitchen cabinets. A small metal chain hit me on the arm as I walked through the dining room into the kitchen.

With flashlights in hand, we slowly walked around the rooms, with me behind Chris. He suddenly jumped back and let out a startled yell as he saw our gold, papier-mache reindeer, which was sitting on the floor in front of the living room fireplace, had moved and was now resting on the lounge chair.

"How did that move?" I asked Chris.

"You're asking me? How should I know?"

A crash came from the kitchen. Startled, we continued to walk slowly through the rooms and hall back to the front door. Our nerves were frazzled by this time. We heard a shuffling noise coming from upstairs. Frightened, I grabbed onto Chris's shoulder as he raised his flashlight towards the sound. Its golden beam of light slowing climbed up the stairs. I think we both stopped breathing. We both screamed and jumped back at the same time as our gaze caught a face staring back at us. There, the large Winnie the Pooh stuffed pillow that Chris had stored in his room had been moved and was now staring down at us from the top of the steps, with its silly grin on his face, leaning on his paws. How could something normally that cute now look so terrifying!

We screamed again.

Jesus! Who moved it?

We listened for more movement but the house was silent and remained in inky blackness. Fumbling through my phone book with my flashlight, I called the power company's emergency number about the outage but it seemed they weren't experiencing any reports of widespread power outages in our neighborhood.

For three hours, we huddled together on the couch without heat in the January cold, wrapped in a large blanket, watching a program on Chris' computer on back-up batteries. The lights from our numerous candles flickered in the room and cast shadows in competition with the shadows of the unknown. We didn't go upstairs until the lights came back on, thankfully, around midnight. We called our next-door neighbors the next day and asked if they knew something about the cause of the blackout but they didn't seem to know anything about it. That was strange. It appeared we were the only ones to experience the blackout.

I wonder to this day if I let something even more sinister into the house when I opened the door. And I feared that the superstition could be true: that an empty knock at the front door brings death to a house.

CHAPTER 4
LIES SWEPT UNDER THE RUG

I did my best to deal with the paranormal activities at Paul's house while there, helped by Chris and the friends who were also witness to it. After all, when it started we found it interesting and even a bit amusing. To see things flying around in a house in the suburbs seemed, at times, like a movie script and we kept peeking into corners to see if there were hidden cameras.

But there was one very sad aspect that only I could deal with and that was Paul's betrayal of trust. I thought he and I had shared the most important parts of our lives, and he was always there with a shoulder to lean on and a kind word as I faced life as a single mom. What I learned in his house made me rethink all that had gone on.

When we first entered the house after his death, we were overwhelmed with the clear evidence that Paul had become a hoarder. From floor to ceiling papers, books, boxes and more scattered about. Walking through his dirty kitchen that had seen cleaner days was shocking. I didn't know any of this, as I'd not visited him in quite a while. This was not the same house I'd had countless dinners in, joining Paul and his parents. What could have happened since the deaths of his parents that changed all that?

I would find that the hoarding was the least of the secrets he was hiding and if Chris had not been extremely diligent in the cleaning out process, I might never have known.

It had been June 15, 2009 and Chris and I were cleaning out Paul's mother's bedroom.

Chris lifted an empty cabinet away from the wall and dragged it across the area carpet.

"What's this?" He asked as he bent down to pick something up. Chris held up a thin black leather booklet that was about the size of a passport with gold embossing on the cover.

"Look, Mom, this was under the carpet that the cabinet was on. Is that a Nazi insignia on it?"

"Let me see."

There was no mistaking the markings on the well-worn dark cover. The embossed area showed the spread wings of an eagle on top of a swastika, the symbol of the German Third Reich.

"Mom, was Mr. Jaeger a Nazi?"

I didn't know. Paul's family emigrated from Germany to the United States in 1949, and he once mentioned his father had been in the Navy but never that he served during World War II, and I never asked. I sat on the bed and scrutinized the booklet. It was some sort of a military I.D. book. It had fewer than fifteen pages total. Inside, on the left hand side, there was a small photo of a young Mr. Jaeger in uniform. On the other pages were ink stamps of dates and locations. I didn't speak or read German but I could make out that it held a list of his inoculations against diseases during his time in the service, which dated from 1941. It stated he was married and that he had a wife, Hilda, and a son. I knew his brother Carl was ten years older than Paul so the year of 1943 given as his birth date made sense.

"I think he was trying to hide that he was a Nazi, Mom. Why do you think it was hidden under the carpet? And why would he keep it?"

"I'm going to show this to your grandfather," I told Chris.

My father had also served in World War II, in the Army Air Corp. He had been a radioman in a ten-member crew on a B-24 Bomber. His Bombardment Group, stationed in Italy, made bombing raids over Germany, Austria and the oil depots in Romania.

When I showed the book to him he didn't hesitate to remark, "That son-of-a-bitch was SS!" He never fully explained how he knew and I was too shocked to argue with him. I couldn't believe it and thought my dad had to be mistaken.

But, perhaps my dad was not mistaken. It was the second weekend in August 2009, when I received a surprise long distance call from a woman named Sylvia Goldberg. I never met her before but I knew she was a good friend of Paul's. She had written a letter to Paul, which had been forwarded to me in July. Inside she had enclosed a group picture of Paul and his mother and Sylvia and her mother. The photo was dated September 2000 and had been taken on Sylvia's mother's 90th birthday. She called to thank me for writing back and sending her the news about Paul. She was sorry to hear of his sudden death.

We chatted for a while and in our conversation Sylvia told me her mother had been a close friend and neighbor of the Jaegers for many years and that Mrs. Jaeger had been very upset when her mother had moved to Maryland to live with her.

"You mentioned in your letter that it's been some time since you were in touch with Paul. How long has it been, Sylvia?"

"It's been several years, but I was thinking about him this past Christmas and wanted to write for the longest time. Our families always spent time together at Christmas, sharing a meal and exchanging gifts. When I came across the picture, I wanted to send it to him. I'm sorry he never got it."

"I'm sorry too; it's a great picture of all of you. You said your mom was a close friend of Mrs. Jaeger?"

"Yes, Hilda and my mom were close friends, which was a bit unusual. We're Jewish and with the Jaegers coming from Germany after World War II, you would think it would have made an awkward relationship. Instead, they bonded over both being immigrants from Europe and the war, and since they both loved sewing and making clothes they became good friends." Sylvia continued, "Hilda Jaeger always contended her family and the German people never knew about what was happening to the Jews during the War. She claimed they were all ignorant of the facts of what happened to the Jewish people until much later when the horrors of the Holocaust came to light."

"Well you must have known how proud Paul was of his German heritage," I said. "He told me about his great-grandfather who received the Iron Cross and other medals in World War I, although he never volunteered much information about his father's involvement during the Second World War. I knew he and his father didn't have a close relationship."

"Well, we called his father 'the mysterious Mr. Jaeger.' Before we moved, Hilda came to visit my mother, knowing it could be the last time she would see her. She told her something she had kept to herself for many years. Hilda cried and confessed to my mother, that the German people did know all along what was happening to the Jews in Europe. She said she was so sorry about the lies and events that led to the Holocaust," Sylvia said. "I think she wanted to clear her conscience. She never saw my mother again and died the following year."

"I don't know what to say, Sylvia. I knew Paul for thirty years and he never let on about any of that. I wonder what else he had been keeping secret about his family all these years."

Then Sylvia told me something that made me almost drop the phone.

"Well you know, Anita, Mr. Jaeger was SS."

I couldn't believe Paul's father, a man I knew for fourteen years before his death in 1993, could be a part of that despicable group. Before I could accept that horrific accusation, I would need to check it out. I was determined to find out more and began my research in this dark chapter in German history.

CHAPTER 5
CONNECTIONS BEING MADE

A white wooden door, the old kind that's real wood, solid throughout and not the cheaper plywood that has become so popular today, is at the top of the stairs leading into my basement. It is the kind of door that is found in many older houses throughout my neighborhood and others like it. But the door in my house is different because it stands between me and the evil at the bottom of my steps. We couldn't see but it had made itself known in vicious ways.

It started only a week after the terrifying blackout, on a snowy January afternoon. I went to the basement to retrieve some books that I was going to donate to charity. I started to move things around to find the plastic bins they were in. I noticed in one of them the same seashell that had flown into the bin at Paul's house was still there, in the bottom. I took it out and as I did, I was overwhelmed with a flood of memories. They were not good memories of that basement. I could still smell the loathsome, moldy stench that permeated the air.

Then, I distinctly heard a loud thump on the side of another plastic bin. Startled, I looked around and decided I wasn't going to move anything else and headed for the stairs. Within seconds,

I found myself in the middle of poltergeist activity. Here we go again! It was just like being in Paul's haunted basement! The dust-pan and broom leaning against the back basement wall fell over by themselves and a green felt tip pen flipped off my large worktable. As I bent to pick up the marker a red tape dispenser flew up to the ceiling, hit the air conditioning duct, and smacked back down again landing hard on the concrete floor. I could feel cold air moving all around me. I became terrified of being in the basement and ran up the stairs as fast as I could as several bottles of cleaner that were stored on the side of the steps, were thrown between the railing and down to the bottom of the basement. I slammed the door shut and vowed it would be awhile before I'd go into the basement again. I knew I needed to get the professionals back to help.

I contacted Laurie and Tri-County Paranormal to tell her of the new activity at our house. She was very sorry to hear of the new spirit trouble but given all that we had been through, and all that she and her team had encountered at Paul's, she wasn't completely surprised. She had warned us this might happen. She told me that she had tried to contact me in late October to see if we were ok, but I never received her email. She quickly set up an appointment to come the following week to investigate our house. I was relieved that they were coming to help validate this new paranormal activity. They had never been to my house and I wondered what could possibly be in store for them.

CHAPTER 6

WHAT DWELT BEFORE

I met Laurie and her team at my front door. It was the evening of January 29 and only nineteen days since we had the terrifying blackout. I was happy to see that Randy, the medium who had channeled Paul during the session at his home, and his wife Clare, another of the team who had been in Paul's house, were with her. Without the three of them, I don't know how we would have been able to successfully finish the "spiritual cleanup" of the house for the estate sale.

It didn't take long for Laurie to have a reaction and she had only walked across the lawn.

"Anita," she said, "you know there's something here already."

I was speechless.

Laurie hadn't even stepped into my house and she was already picking up on something unnatural.

"Before this new activity you told me about, didn't you ever pick up on anything strange going on in your house?"

"Not really," I answered her. I was surprised she would ask, as I have lived in my home for over twenty-three years and never had anything strange occur. We had heard sounds on occasion but my house is old and we attributed it to that. I certainly had never felt threatened and I never dreamed our house could be haunted or produce paranormal activity.

My house did, however, have a very interesting story. I had been a member of our local historical society and had looked up the land's long history.

My Cape Cod-style house was built on the remains of an 1800's farmhouse. The property had been continually occupied by early Welsh settlers starting in the late 1700's and was then owned by one family until the 1870's when the second family took over the property. In fact, I saw an old map of our neighborhood from 1922 that showed only trees and just a stone foundation of the old farmhouse. By the 1940's, the land was sold in pieces for housing developments and my house was constructed in 1947, directly over the original foundation of the old farmhouse.

We still had the remains of the original fireplace in our basement, which had been reconstructed using some of the old bricks and mortar along with newer cinder blocks, a new flue, a metal framed firebox and screen. The previous owner who had built the Cape Cod was able to use the fireplace on cold winter days when he worked in the basement as a leather craftsman. What was curious was that in front of the old fireplace was a section of the original dirt floor that the poured modern concrete floor did not cover. I never understood why it was left that way.

Outside of the house, Chris and I were always finding artifacts: pottery, a silver spoon, hand-forged spikes, and some square head nails while doing yard work. Through the years, I personally had found porcelain cup handles, pieces of glazed stoneware, shards of colored glass and parts of dishes with blue designs on them. We discovered possible signs of Native American habitation when, after a hard rain, Chris found obsidian chips that looked hand-worked. I just thought this stuff was so interesting and with me being such a history buff, I kept many of the items in cans and jars. My mother would just shake her head and call it junk.

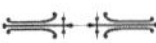

It was time to get to work. Laurie's team did an initial sweep and a reading with their EMF detector around the house and they finally stopped at the top of the steps to the basement. EMF devices measure ambient (surrounding) electromagnetic fields. Laurie had explained to Chris and me back at Paul's house that this was a very important piece of equipment that ghost researchers used as a tracking device. It is a common theory among paranormal researchers that spirits disrupt this electromagnetic field and that you can tell one is present by higher than normal readings with this meter. The units of measure most often used for an EMF meter in the U.S.A. are called milligaus (mg). A normal reading is a 1.0 or lower base line. A paranormal occurrence or ghost may give off milligaus readings in the range of 1.5 mg to about 6 mg depending on the EMF meter you use. Fluctuations of 2.0 to 7.0 could indicate spirit presence.

Laurie and her team were aware of the hundreds of boxes of collectibles and artifacts that I had taken from Paul's house that were now making a home here. I didn't like the huge clutter but I had no choice at the time. I needed to remove the items from Paul's house as soon as possible because of time constraints dealing with the estate's beneficiaries. I had no other place to put the items until the estate was settled. With my finances stretched thin, I had little money left over to rent storage units each month to house all the items. My near empty basement seemed the logical choice. To say this was a supremely bad decision would be a huge understatement.

Laurie suggested to her team to start there. I led them down the stairs as Chris followed us with his camcorder to capture the session. Laurie and her team became excited when they got some high hits on the EMF detector on a Peruvian mummy doll, an American Indian spear point and some pottery in one of the boxes. The label on the spear point stated that it came from a graveyard. Paul had either bought or dug these up years ago but there wasn't anything else to identify it inside the box or give me a clue where it originally came from.

Laurie put her meter up to the spear point. The needle jumped several degrees.

"Wow, Clare do you see this?" Clare went over with her separate meter and saw her needle also jump. They next placed their meters over a piece of pottery.

"OH MY GOSH!" exclaimed Laurie. "My meter is going crazy. Point 6, point 9, 1 point 5, 2 point 0, 2 point 7, 2 point 9! This shouldn't be happening."

Randy walked around to the bottom of the steps and gave us his impression on what was happening in the basement. He said that he saw two, and then three separate spirit groups near the steps. Chris later saw that he had captured on his video that, at the moment Randy mentioned the groups of spirits, white balls of energy or "orbs," which are considered by some as possible manifestations of spirit energy, were coming out from the stairs and swirling around Laurie and Randy. They seemed to linger for a moment and then they quickly darted away. Whether you believe in orbs as spirits or not, it was very coincidental that Chris captured them at the very moment Randy seemed to make spirit contact.

That was not the only thing that was caught on Laurie's digital devices. As we stood near the back shelves of the basement where boxes of Paul's items were stored, Laurie asked several questions while holding her digital recorder.

"Who are you? Are you the one causing the activity here?"

"I don't wanna.....Huuuuumph... shhhh... click, click, click."

It sounded as if something was first reluctant to answer and annoyed with her question. *Something* was the right word. Laurie said it gave her chills.

"Who is the oldest spirit in this house?" Clare asked.

Static..."the boy... first." (We would not know of the importance of this EVP – Electronic Voice Phenomenon - until months later and realize what a significant piece of evidence Laurie captured on tape).

"There is a column of energy that goes straight up to the first floor where things get thrown in the hallway," Randy pointed out. "It's very powerful."

Randy sat down on the bottom steps and appeared tired. After another fifteen minutes went by and he didn't pick up anything further, Laurie and Claire also appeared weary and they headed back upstairs.

"Is it Paul?" I asked Randy as we returned to the living room and sat down on the couches.

"Paul is not here Anita, but what I've made contact with are inter-dimensional beings and they are frantic and very afraid that the artifact will fall into the wrong hands. They need you to find it."

"You mean the item "not of this world?" I asked him in earnest. "Inter-dimensional beings are here *now*? But we don't even know what this *object* looks like for God's sake."

"They know you are starting to write a book about them and they don't like it, Anita," Laurie interjected.

"That's just too damn bad they don't like it!" I was angry. "They *all* should have left us alone. Don't you understand how crazy this all sounds? Some of own family members and friends don't believe me. If I write this down somehow it makes sense to me and validates that this really happened. I have to write this because if I don't, I'll regret it for the rest of my life!"

No one said a word as they waited for me to calm down. Laurie continued with her analysis that whatever once peacefully cohabitated with us in our house was now mad at us for bringing in something malevolent with Paul's artifacts.

"They are telling me, Anita, that they were minding their own business here but once you brought in the dark energy with all Paul's stuff they are now having a fit!"

"There is a war going on. The 'artifact' or the object 'not of this world' emits a power and has opened a portal in your house," Randy stated. "It's a 'free for all' for spirits, a terminal now for the dead to pass through."

"What kind of energy? Is it dangerous?" I was growing more alarmed by the minute.

"I believe that the energy the object emits could have had something to do with Paul's early and untimely death," Randy said. "Remember the 'object' changes shapes to protect itself and you should now be looking for something that may look like a large coin with a man's head on it."

How did that help I wondered? Many coins have heads of men on them. What would make *this* stand out from the others?

Laurie suggested we start looking through the boxes to see what we could find. We were perplexed and I asked Laurie's team, "How does one find something that changes shapes and colors and doesn't want to be found?"

Randy became silent, deep in thought. No one had an answer for us. They had never encountered anything like this in an investigation. I felt frustrated and angry to be left with this ongoing mystery and did not know what dangerous consequences would play out in my home.

Before leaving Randy warned us, "Be careful guys, something very dark and evil has been unleashed here. Call if you need us."

They packed up their equipment and said they would be back soon for a further investigation.

They left us with more questions than answers, and I felt guilty because I had brought evil to my basement.

CHAPTER 7
SPIRITED VISITORS

It's bad enough when your house – your sanctuary, the place where you can escape the crazy world – becomes home to evil spirits. It's disconcerting at best when you have to wonder if the noises in the night are because of the wind or because an unseen visitor is present and watching. As a child you wondered if there was something hiding under your bed but hiding under the covers and calling mom or dad could solve that.

What is worse, though, is when the evil spirits chase you into your dreams and sleep becomes not a refuge or recharging of the body but a frightening, inescapable journey. How do you escape that? There aren't enough bed covers in the world.

For Chris, this problem became all too real. Night after night he would be visited in his dreams by people he didn't know but who, we would find, were connected to everything that was going on in the haunting we faced.

It started out with a vivid dream Chris had of Paul only a few weeks after his sudden death in 2009. I was at the breakfast table paying bills and Chris came downstairs. He looked like something was bothering him as he headed into the living room to his worktable. I watched as he began to paint one of his Warhammer models. He was silent but I could tell he had something on his mind.

"Chris, would you like some breakfast? It's not a good idea to skip it."

"I'll have an early lunch," he said, without looking up or at me.

A mother's intuition, call it. I knew that something big was on his mind.

He didn't look up, but just spoke. "By the way, Paul says 'Hi.'"

Surprised, I stopped what I was doing and looked up at him. "What are you talking about?"

He kept his head bent over the model, deep in concentration.

"I saw Paul last night in a dream that really didn't feel like a dream. It was very vivid. He was sitting across from me on the recliner in this room, dressed in a red hoodie and dark brown pants. He told me he was at the memorial service and that you'd done a great job. He really liked it."

I just stared at Chris.

"He also said to me that a massive cleanup seemed to be underway at his house and he was saddened that things were being changed."

I was stunned. "Are you kidding me?"

"No, I'm not kidding, Mom. Paul's face looked gray and he told me that he'd been a bit scattered lately and it had taken a while for him to get his energy back."

I couldn't believe what I was hearing because it sounded just like Paul to use a pun like 'being scattered' when he knew full well that his last wishes were to have his ashes scattered on a mountain top out west, as they had been only days earlier. I guess I was feeling a little hurt that my friend hadn't come to me.

"I wonder why he came to you and not me," I said.

"He came to me because he knows how mad you are at him. He figured you didn't want to see him."

I put my hand to my mouth. "Oh my God!"

Chris continued, "He seemed to think like there was nothing wrong, and in his mind it was business as usual and that he was going home after our visit. Then, he said, 'I'll see you again,' and I told him, 'Dude, you're dead.' He didn't say anything; he just got up from the chair and walked right through the wall."

My jaw dropped.

"Mom, I feel so drained this morning, like I didn't get any sleep at all last night."

"I don't know what to say, Chris," I said, as chills ran up my spine. Then I had a creepy thought. Of course, Paul's complexion looked gray; he had been cremated, hadn't he?

It was a startling occurrence, to say the least, but I wasn't totally surprised. There was no doubt in my mind that my son's long-time connection to Paul and his involvement in cleaning out his house had somehow triggered and brought out a dormant psychic ability that had always been present.

Looking back, I remember a young Chris telling me of an imaginary friend that played with him in his bedroom. He called him "Jolly Bear" and would make playdough pizzas for him. Chris never told me of any unusual dreams before this one but he did go through a period of time when he was about six years old, when he would awake in the middle of the night, come into my bedroom frightened and tell me, "the lady was looking at me." At first, I thought it was my Renaissance woman's portrait hanging in the hall near his bedroom. I removed it thinking that was the cause of his terror. I never considered that it could have been something else.

I had recently come across an old school journal that Chris had kept for a grammar school assignment. I had been rummaging in my hall desk for a copy book when I found it. It was marked

1991 and Chris had drawn on the cover, ironically, one of his favorite characters from the Ghostbusters movie. The crude figure was drawn in pencil and wore a uniform with the famous backpack the Ghostbusters wore to fight and capture ghosts. Chuckling, I took a few moments to enjoy looking through these early writings and observations my son made when he was eight years old. In the middle of the book there was a curious entry written in October, 1991. Chris wrote, "It's raining outside and the sly thing is under my bed." The sly thing? What could he have possibly been talking about? Perhaps "Jolly Bear" wasn't so jolly?

Chris was also dreaming of people he never met, who turned out to be historical figures.

One of the first of these people to visit Chris in a dream was a fellow by the name of Luke Short. Chris handed me a piece of paper with that name on it one day soon after the first dream. I had never heard of him but Chris told me the man had worked with the lawman and writer, Bat Masterson, who I had heard of. But he didn't know much more so we did some research on the internet.

In *Luke Short: A Biography by Wayne Short,* I read that Short was called a "'jack-of-all trades' – an Old West gunfighter who was also a farmer, cowboy, whiskey peddler, army scout, dispatch rider, gambler and even a saloon keeper at times. In his lifetime of less than four decades, he became associated with Wyatt Earp, a name known to many. He was known for being a man of few words and being good with a gun. A fastidious dresser he was no slouch with a six-shooter, either." This enigmatic man was close friends with Bat Masterson and Wyatt Earp and shot it out with some of the deadliest gunmen of that era. When he died of congestive heart failure in 1893, he was only thirty-nine years old. Why did this man appear in Chris's dream? Like Luke Short, Paul had also been involved in a variety of personal and business pursuits: a writer, lecturer, explorer of sorts and collector of historic items. He was a man who dressed well and died of a sudden heart attack too. What was the connection, we wondered.

More long-dead people came to Chris in dreams in the following weeks. There was the morning

Chris woke up and asked me if I ever heard of Enid. No, I hadn't, I told him. He then told me a WW II pilot, whose name was Lt. Robert Strickler and who lost his life in the South Pacific in World War II, came to him. He was in Enid.

We looked up Enid on the internet and found that Enid was a town in Oklahoma and there was a large cemetery there. On the cemetery's website I found this description of notable people interred there:

> "There are several grave markers that contribute to the historic significance of the cemetery: William F. Svarik (1909) in the Catholic cemetery, W.C. Conley (1889-1921) in Potter's Field, William Mason (1909-1936) and M.J. Adler (1867-1919), in the Jewish section, Lt. Commander Robert L. Strickler killed in action."

There he was. Officer Lt. Robert Strickler, the person who came to Chris in his dream. First, a colorful character from the old west appeared to Chris and now a pilot from World War II? What was the relevance?

I started to research to learn more about why this might be happening. When we dream we are very open to communication from deceased loved ones and from the other side because in our sleep state we visit the astral planes, a non-physical place or plane of existence.

> In a way, it's like a halfway house between the spiritual and the physical. When you leave your body at night and visit the astral planes, you experience what it is like to be alive but not in a body. It's easier for the deceased 'to meet us half-way' energetically speaking, by visiting us there. Because the astral plane is like a half-way house between heaven (the ether) and Earth, dreams are an important part of our spiritual life – something that keeps us connected to spirit. Therefore dreaming is an easy way for spirit to get a message to you.
>
> *(Source: http://annasayce.com/how-to-interpret-your-dreams)*

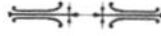

Chris definitely was having spirits visit him, even the spirits of people he'd never met.

Chris will tell you he is a very reluctant psychic. He wished he didn't have dead people coming to him in the middle of the night giving him messages for hours that leave him tired and drained of energy in the morning. But he has always been intellectually curious and seemed to be taking it all with a good nature. He even showed his sense of humor, jokingly saying that he certainly was making our lives very spirited and interesting!

However, as his mother, I worried about the dark along with the light that seemed attracted to him. I wanted to support him, as I believed him to be truly gifted and a sensitive with special abilities. Having this psychic ability in some ways was a blessing but as Chris so colorfully put it, "A pain in the ass!"

CHAPTER 8

A PENNY FOR YOUR THOUGHTS?

I've run my own business, Past Images by Anita, for many years. It's been based out of my home office and I often have clients visit. Apparently the spirits in the house thought it would be entertaining to act up when some of those clients came by.

It was January 20, and one day past the anniversary of Paul's death, when they made themselves quite known.

An elderly client, Mrs. Sterns, had come to pick up the antique dolls that I restored for her. She seemed fascinated with some of the unusual experiences I'd had at Paul's.

We talked at the dining room table while I served some tea and she said in all her almost ninety years she had never witnessed any type of ghostly activity, although in her Jewish religion, angels were prevalent and appeared in their scared books, which I was not aware. I asked her if she believed in an afterlife when we suddenly heard something drop in the living room. Chris was sitting on the couch working at his laptop when he called out to me that something hard had landed near the TV. We both went over to the TV and discovered a penny. It appeared to have dropped from the ceiling onto the TV stand! My shocked client came into the room as I slowly walked around the room.

BANG!

Something hit the doorframe to my studio. I checked it out and lying on the floor was a painted Warhammer figurine, its paint chipped from the force of the throw. This made Chris very angry.

"What are they throwing now?" Chris asked. "Of course! More of *my* stuff!"

Mrs. Sterns look concerned but didn't say anything.

BANG!

Something else hit the kitchen doorframe. It was another Warhammer figurine but this was an unpainted one.

"Why are they doing this and with my guys?" shouted Chris.

He was particularly confused as these figurines were not upstairs on his art table with the other figurines. These had been packed away in plastic bins in the basement.

My client sat at the dining room table again and was in a state of disbelief over what just happened. She had heard the poltergeist activity herself and could only shake her head in amazement. She finished her tea and before she left, she went back into the living room to say goodbye to Chris.

A white fabric bow lay on the carpet in the center of the room. Chris hadn't noticed this as he was so engrossed at his computer screen and hadn't heard a thing. We chuckled with nervous amazement as we looked further and saw a line of lace and bows in a row up to the front living room windows. I recognized the trimmings of white and purple bows, yellow lace and tan ribbons that Paul had given me to use for my doll costumes. They had been tucked away in a portable bin with drawers where I kept my sewing items, located on the side of the living room. I also found a white metal hook used for a doll's umbrella that had been thrown in the hallway below the steps. I remembered finding it at Paul's house and thought to keep it to use if I ever made a doll parasol. It had also been in a drawer in the same bin.

Mrs. Sterns stood incredulous as she remembered there had been nothing on the rug only minutes before.

"Oy vey!" These were the only words I understood in the flood of expressive Yiddish that came out of the poor frightened woman's mouth. When my client was leaving I got the distinct feeling that she wouldn't be coming back to visit my house anytime soon as she kept repeating that she had never experienced anything like this in her long life. She was very concerned for me and as she gave me a big hug, I could tell she was shaking!

CHAPTER 9
A SCARY WARNING

I remember things appearing and disappearing at Paul's house and that caused us much frustration when we were trying to locate and pack the hundreds of items he had left. Now different things were starting to disappear in my house. Money and other objects were evaporating into thin air.

There was a time one evening when Chris had some tools on his work table disappear and we spent the better part of an hour in the living room, looking for his files and paint brushes. I looked under my recliner and found to my astonishment an old tarnished liquid silver and turquoise bead necklace. I didn't remember owning such a necklace and could not understand how it got there.

"GIVE THEM BACK, GODDAMMIT!" Chris yelled in desperation to the ghostly tricksters. We finally found the tools under the coffee table but knew they had just been returned as we had looked under that table several times.

Chris experienced his cell phone disappearing another time, called his number from another phone and heard it ring in the ether but his search turned up nothing. The next morning it appeared on the dining room table. His girlfriend Heather, who later became his wife, remembers the incident clearly and to this day still talks about this strange incident.

On a day in February, which happened to be St. Valentine's Day, (one of Paul's favorite historical saints that he wrote about many times) I decided to take my digital recorder in the basement. I was hoping I could make contact with whatever was doing the stealing. I needed my money back!

I placed the recorder on a box and began to ask a series of questions, directing them to Paul and any members of his family who might be present in the basement. An unexpected wave of sadness came over me. Keeping my composure I spoke aloud. "Why are items disappearing from my house and who is moving them?" I waited. There was nothing but silence.

Again, this time I spoke directly to Paul with the questions for which I most wanted an answer.

"What was the object we took out of your home that you were so concerned about? Was this object 'not of this world' here now in my basement? Is this object the reason for our new and increasing paranormal activity?" Again nothing

I tried again with my next question. "Is there anyone who would like to talk with me?"

Suddenly, my heater went on and it started making a loud humming noise. I decided to quit because the noise was going to taint any further EVP recording. I spoke aloud once more, telling the recorder that the heater was making too much noise and that I would be going back upstairs. Then, after looking around the space for a few more moments, I climbed the stairs up to the dining room.

Chris and I began to listen to the nine and one-half minute recording. At first, we heard only static and a few light bumps and taps, but no voices or sounds to answer my first questions. I was disappointed because I was beginning to realize how important the "object" was and how critical it was for us to find it.

But while there were no answers, we did hear that the audio became noticeably louder although I did not turn the volume up when I directed my questions to Paul. I had put the recorder down on a box the whole time and never touched it; something else turned up the volume dial on its own.

To my question about whether anyone wanted to communicate, Chris and I both heard what we thought might be a response but it was neither clear or loud enough to be sure. We jotted down the time and what we thought we heard in the recording so we could do a second review later.

We were just about done our review when suddenly, right near the end as I said into the recorder I would be going upstairs, we heard the most horrible EVP of a growling, inhuman voice commanding me to what sounded like "SHUT OFF THE RECORDER!"

What?

We rewound the last part and listened again.

"SHUT OFF THE RECORDER!"

It scared the hell out of us! But on the tape, there is no sign that I reacted, just the sound of me walking up the wooden steps. I didn't react because I did not hear the voice, but whatever made the sound had to be close to me. I was shaken to the core when I heard the tape and the voice – it sounded like this thing had been right next to me.

Thank goodness my washer and dryer were in my kitchen because I didn't go down the basement again for quite a while.

CHAPTER 10

MARCH MADNESS

I always knew that I had to tell my story of the paranormal experiences we had at Paul's. I'd been enthralling people about them and even with the many witnesses we had, there were people looking at me like I was crazy. Or worse, I was making the whole thing up. It was one thing if people thought I was a liar but I couldn't allow that to happen to Chris or the friends and family who came to help us.

It was March 12 of 2010 when I sat down in front of my computer and began writing the manuscript for my book, *Estate of Horror.* I had decided in January to write my story but I always hesitated, thinking it might not be the right thing. But with all the new activity, I knew it was time. Now, it was actually happening. After experiencing the unexplainable and the ordeal with the paranormal, I knew I had to record the extraordinary haunted experiences that Chris, I, and other witnesses saw and heard on our audio and video equipment.

My friends and family members, many who were in Paul's house with us or who heard of the unusual events happening at the estate, urged me to write a book. However, at first, I did not intend to write it myself. I felt if I provided the story and the materials, even possibly be interviewed, then someone else could do a better job. Having no formal experience other than a creative writing class in high school and a one-act play I wrote for a college assignment (ironically about a revengeful ghost) I was on the learning curve.

I was at my computer writing one day when I heard a buzz coming from upstairs and thought Chris was shaving. Then I heard Chris call to me from the living room.

"What's that noise?"

"That's not you?" I asked.

I followed the sound and went upstairs to find that Chris' electric toothbrush was turned on. Now this is not easily turned on and Chris hadn't been up there recently. This was not the first time I had heard his electric toothbrush turn on by itself. This had happened about three times in the past few months. He was out one night and I was watching TV when I heard a buzzing noise. I finally turned down the TV and realized the noise wasn't the program. I went upstairs and sure enough, it was his electric toothbrush vibrating on the sink's counter top. Do ghosts need to brush their teeth in the afterlife?

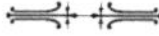

A week later a very good client of mine, Ann Marie Pelosi, came to pick up her restored photos. I had known Ann Marie for a number of years and had done many photo restorations for her family. As we sat in my studio and talked about Paul and my work as his executor, I heard a bang in the hallway. I tried to ignore it as we continued our conversation.

BANG! CLANG! BANG!

There was no ignoring the loud sound as multiple objects hit the outside wall of my studio that faced our center hallway.

Ann Marie's eyes grew wide in surprise. "Oh my God Anita, what was that?"

Chris called out from his upstairs bedroom, "What's going on down there?"

I went in the hallway and found four German Deutsche Marks lying on the carpet. Three of them were from the year 1949 and one was from 1953. I immediately realized that these dates coincided with the dates Paul's family came to the United States from Germany in 1949 – and the year Paul was born in the U.S. in 1953. They had come from the direction of the living room.

Chris yelled down to me once more. He had a small stuffed animal of the TV cartoon character ALF in his room; it was now in the empty clothesbasket in the hallway. He had not put it there. Taking it from the clothesbasket, Chris walked back to his room. There he saw that his Gizmo puppet was stuck up in his ceiling fan. This puppet had been in Paul's collection; was he now saying "Hi" to us on St. Patrick's Day, which happened to be another one of his favorite holidays?

Anne Marie went upstairs to see Gizmo stuck in my son's ceiling fan and came down bewildered and shaking her head.

"I knew what you said before about your friend's house being haunted was the truth, Anita, but now I really believe you!"

"Yeah, it may be leprechauns having a field day with us Ann Marie!"

She gave me a big hug, told me to be careful, and soon left. I wasn't sure she'd want to come back to my house anytime soon.

My thoughts of Ann Marie not returning to my house turned out to be prophetic. I never did see Ann Marie in person again. She was in touch with me after being diagnosed with pancreatic cancer which shocked and saddened me. I mailed her a copy of *Estate of Horror* when it was published and she was so happy she got to read that book, which occupied her during some of her treatments. Ann Marie put up a valiant fight for almost two years but passed away December 2014. Unfortunately, my cousin Ellen who died November 2013 from brain cancer never had a chance to read

Estate of Horror. Both these women will always be an inspiration to me in the way they lived their lives and courageously faced a deadly foe.

The tricks kept coming as another strange thing happened that same afternoon.

I was talking to another client on my phone about picking up a restored doll, a surprise for his wife's birthday, when suddenly an orange blur went flashing by, down the hallway stairs. I hung up quickly and found a red nylon scrubby that had been in the kitchen sink had been thrown from upstairs and hit my flower basket in the hallway. Damaged blossoms from the dried flowers lay scattered on the carpet. I was puzzled. How did the orange scrubby get upstairs for *them* to throw it downstairs! I yelled out to the spirits, "Cut it out and stop ruining my flowers! Get an afterlife and stop bothering me!" They took the hint for a few quiet hours.

The tricks and March madness continued. That evening, while Chris' girlfriend Heather ate in the dining room after a long day at work, she heard along with me, objects thrown down the steps hitting the front door.

CLANG!

"NOT AGAIN!" yelled Chris from upstairs. He had been getting ready for their date. "What got thrown now?"

I ran over to see what the objects were and found five foreign coins on the rug. Heather looked at me inquisitively but didn't seem to be too shaken by this occurrence. She herself has been sensitive all her life and knew about our house from Chris. When she and Chris started dating he told her about the episodes with the paranormal we were experiencing, his apparent psychic abilities and what we had been through the previous year at Paul's house. She was unfazed when Chris told her these things and she mentioned to him that she *too* was familiar with hauntings as she believed her mother's house to be haunted while she was growing up. She recalled how she hated to be alone at her house, as she'd hear her name being called, especially when in the shower. She had experienced dreams in the past that seemed to come true and she believed that one of her grandmothers guards her, as her mother still keeps that grandmother's ashes in the house. As she and Chris continued to date, Heather accepted that she was not in a normal relationship. After all, her boyfriend speaks to the dead!

CHAPTER 11

END OF AN ERA

The contractors had renovated Paul's house through the harsh winter of 2010 and contacted us to ask if we'd like to stop by to see the new improvements. They let Chris and I walk through the newly refurbished house and we couldn't believe the changes: a beautifully appointed galley kitchen, sparkling gray and white marbleized tiled bathrooms, fresh, neutral paint and crown moldings on all the walls, shiny refinished wood floors, new windows that you *could* open, and the front enclosed porch taken out and left open, like its original 1950's design. There were also new electric garage doors and a fresh coat of paint on the garden house, which were a vast improvement. The biggest surprise was the basement, as they made a large, spacious carpeted media room out of it. It was no longer the dark, rank smelling and dirty place it once was only 6 months before. We could not believe it was the same basement!

We were surprised to see one strange item left, though. There was a small room partitioned off as a work/laundry room and the contractors had elected to keep Mr. Jaeger's old woodwork bench. Chris and I looked at each other and wondered if this retained any psychic energy for activity in the future for the new owners.

As we walked around the basement I asked Chris what he felt and he told me that there seemed to be very little psychic energy left at the house.

"Sure, it's all at our house now," I said.

When we went back upstairs, we saw an empty light bulb cardboard sleeve lying on the kitchen floor, unusual since the whole place was spotless and there was no trash anywhere.

As we walked on cardboard sheets throughout the house, so as not to scratch the new hardwood floors, we spotted a sand block just lying in the corner of the living room. There was no reason for that to be there either as the room was completely finished.

Chris just looked at me and shook his head. "I'm glad I'm not going to live here."

The contractors didn't seem to have any problems when they worked there those six months to fix the house. A few months later, a young couple from out of town bought it. I never heard anything unusual from the lawyer who handled the estate or the contractors who sold the house. I've talked to Barbara, Paul's neighbor, who lived behind his property several times and she told me the house has been resold again to another older couple who have been doing new landscaping and installed a privacy fence around the property. She was upset that the large tree in Paul's backyard, the one he loved so much, was cut down to make way for a new outdoor deck. So far, she hadn't heard any disturbances from the new neighbors but she was sure Paul wouldn't have been happy over these new changes.

Change had never been easy for my departed friend. Paul was the type of person who would have been comfortable living a hundred years earlier in a more gentile and mannered society. I remember his mother telling me how, when Paul was first teaching history at a local high school, he was shocked by some female students who were quite forward in their intentions to know him better and at some of the coarse language they used. He was not comfortable in that atmosphere and left his teaching position a few years later to pursue work as a guide for the National Park Service in Philadelphia. He was also in charge of their historical costume department. One Halloween he and I went to a party dressed in authentically created Colonial outfits that Paul borrowed for the evening. I wore a full gown and dust cap and Paul looked splendid in wool waistcoat, knee britches, and tri-corner hat. We won for best costumes at the party!

Later Paul worked as an assistant professor of anthropology at a western university and it was there that he really was in his element. His love of ancient Native American culture spanning both North and South America had him working on archaeological sites in the Yucatan, Mexico, and Guatemala and then in Southwest United States where he and his team uncovered an ancient Indian burial ground under an old pioneer town they were excavating. He actually had to give up his research on the ancient Mayan culture while in Guatemala because of rebel activity that made it too dangerous for Americans to stay. He was heartbroken that his dream was interrupted but found solace when the old town in Southern Utah he was transferred to turned up the exciting discovery of the ancient Native American burial ground underneath. He was over the moon when he called to tell me the good news.

That is what Paul and I shared. It was a common bond of love and understanding of the past, its history and all its mysteries and stories to uncover. And if you think it was only a serious nature that made up my friends sole personality you would be mistaken. He was fun to be around. He had a quirky sense of humor and loved puns. He refused to get an answering machine but had caller ID. When he saw it was me calling he would pretend he was a recorded message and say something like, “I’m not here right now. I have traveled back to ancient Greece to interview Socrates. Please leave a message and I'll get back to you some millennium, beep!" Then we would start laughing.

He insisted on writing his various interesting articles on historical topics for the local paper first hand written and then transcribed to an old typewriter. There was no way he was using a computer.

"I am holding out for the written word," he'd say. Paul would Xerox his copies, send one by mail or would hand-deliver one to the publication department. Much to his detriment, and with me warning him that access to a computer would make his life easier, others used fax machines and email to send their e-file articles to the newspapers before he was finished. It was too late when he realized he was putting himself out of freelance work and business.

But that was Paul, a man out of place in this century. He was a man who loved to dig in the past for historical artifacts and I was a person who loved history and restored artifacts. Perhaps that was why we were such great friends.

There is no place to visit Paul in a cemetery and place flowers. His last wishes were that he be cremated. I'd like to think that when his ashes were spread out on the mountain top out west that a small particle of him may have traveled on a windy easterly storm back here to me.

CHAPTER 12
APRIL FOOLS?

Chris suddenly yelled from upstairs. "What the hell?"

He came rushing down the stairs, and I spotted a misty film on his black T-shirt. I tried to brush it off. It left a streak where the dark shirt showed underneath. Was this ectoplasm that I had read about in one of Laurie Hull's paranormal books? She described a similar encounter with this misty type matter that appeared and then disappeared on her shirt while she investigated a haunted location in one of her books. Chris went back upstairs to get a towel from the clothesbasket in the hallway to wipe it off.

He grabbed the clean towel and as he did, the clothesbasket jumped up and enclosed over top of his 5' 10" frame. He was so startled that he fell down all 13 of our carpeted steps with the basket still on his head.

Hearing the terrible thuds, I let out a scream, "What happened, Chris?"

Chris lay at the bottom of the stairs, underneath the plastic clothesbasket. He just shook his head.

Dennis, my ex-boyfriend, was having a sandwich in my living room and watching the news when we both heard and saw a keychain fly down the steps. Dennis was moving to Florida and

Chris was purchasing his car as Dennis was only taking his truck. He now walked over to Chris and asked the all-time supremely intelligent question.

"What happened, did you fall down the stairs?"

"Yeah, you big oaf. It's my lot in life to luge down the stairs with a fucking clothesbasket on my head," Chris replied sarcastically.

Chris got up and assured me he wasn't hurt, the steps were carpeted, and all I could do was shake my head in bewilderment and go back upstairs with the clothesbasket.

A short while later, while I was on the phone in my studio with my insurance agent to transfer the car title I saw Chris frantically motioning me to get off the phone.

"What Chris?" I put my hand over the phone.

"You've got to see what is going on in the living room, Mom."

I hung up as soon as I could and went to the living room. The area looked ransacked. There were objects everywhere: fleece throws from the couches, pillows tossed around and my National Geographic magazines toppled over their rack near the fireplace.

"When did this all happen?" I asked. I was only on the phone a few minutes.

Chris quickly got his digital camera out and snapped some photos of the pile of magazines tossed to one side of the fireplace and captured two anomalies. One picture showed a white streak coming across half the photo near one of the pillows, and in the next photo there was a complete white-out or blob blocking the entire image. The rest of the photos were normal.

As Chris and Dennis walked into the center hall, Chris let out a surprised yell as a handful of paper clips got thrown at his face. Big, brave Dennis ran like hell back to the breezeway, chased outside by a sponge from the sink and a handful of coins.

I continued the "haunted tour" of my own house and found yellow birthday candles scattered all around the dining room, which were taken from the still closed kitchen cabinets.

The poltergeist activity was constant and continued until we couldn't take it anymore. We drove Dennis back to his apartment and left everything the way it was. All this happened within an hour and half but it seemed so much longer. I think my ex-boyfriend was glad he was moving far away from me and my crazy house.

CHAPTER 13
EVIL BELOW

I emailed Laurie and Tri-County Paranormal about the new heavy poltergeist activity happening again in the house and she promised they would try to come as soon as they could.

About a week later, on April 20, her team of investigators came to my house again but this time they got much more in the way of their own personal encounters with the paranormal. Laurie's colleague, Mark, was main camera operator; Beth, who was a new member, made up the team with Laurie.

The team set up some REM-Pods on the floor of our dining room and set up a video camera in the hallway facing the stairs. The pods are the size of a hockey puck and are lighted discs that turn green for normal energy fields and turn red hot when there is electrical or magnetic energy (spirit activity) manifesting near the pods.

They placed their digital recorders, computer, video equipment and cables on my dining room table as a command center.

After going through the living and dining rooms and back to the center hall to get a sense of what was stirring in the atmosphere, Laurie said she felt compelled to go down to the basement. I led them down the stairs and sat down while the rest of the team took positions near the back of the basement. They proceeded to conduct their investigation with their equipment which included an EMF detector, digital cameras, EVP recorders, and infrared camera. With them they would try to make contact with whatever could be lurking in the basement. Mark took some flash pictures around the rooms. . Things were quiet and Laurie asked a series of questions: Who or what was there, and why had they had taken up residence in my basement? Things turned ugly quickly. It seemed Laurie was successful in making contact with a spirit of a dark and evil nature. She suddenly turned to me and told me to leave immediately and go back upstairs. She said I could be in danger. I was at first reluctant to leave but seeing how insistent she was and the fear on her face I didn't argue with her and I went upstairs.

"What's going on Mom?" asked Chris.

I shook my head as I heard loud talking down the basement and wondered what Laurie had tapped into and had felt was so threatening that she needed me to leave.

Several tense moments later, the team came running up the stairs, and we could feel a large cold draft coming up with them. Laurie seemed shaken and pale.

"Oh, my God! I can't believe what just happened!" Laurie appeared out of breath and was rubbing the base of her neck. I could see what looked like red marks there.

Two of the little REM-Pods placed by the team earlier turned red in the dining room and in the hallway. Looking pale and alarmed Laurie tried to explain what had happened in the basement when suddenly Chris and Heather yelled and jumped off the couch.

"Did you see that?" Chris yelled.

A tall shadow figure had appeared in the dining room right in their line of sight. Suddenly, the plastic cover over the large portrait of Paul, taken from his home, was ripped off violently. Luckily Laurie's recorder on the dining room table was still on and captured an EVP. A deep male voice was heard saying in a mocking tone, "I now present Paul Jaeger!" and then you could hear the sound of the cover being ripped off and the reaction of Chris and Heather yelling. Laurie and Beth were both shocked – they did not remember Paul's last name but could now make it out on the EVP. We were surprised by this revelation and wondered why Paul's picture was being targeted.

After we settled down a few minutes, Laurie revealed that there seemed to be an evil and dark presence in the basement. When Laurie asked him and pressed further where *he* was from, he said he was from Hell.

"He was going to hurt you, Anita and that's why we sent you upstairs."

"Oh my God, Laurie," I cried and put my arms around her.

Laurie said it tried to scare her by threatening to strangle her. The images, she said, that flooded her mind, were of a pornographic and sick, murderous nature as she first saw the killing of women and children by strangulation and then us too!

Marks's camera suddenly made a noise and stopped working. He went to check on it where he had set it up in the hallway earlier.

Laurie sat on the bottom of the hallway stairs trying to regain her composure. She said she could feel a little child's presence and that they were afraid of the "bad man in the basement." It possibly explained the child-like antics happening in our house – like someone running up the stairs and throwing down objects for fun. Laurie said the "ghost child" felt safe and stayed in Chris' room because of the fun toys there.

"Has this little child ever come to you in a dream, Chris?"

Chris nodded. "I did see a child in a dream and I sensed he was scared."

"Jesus, it's fried!" Mark yelled out loud. All his recordings for the last several hours were gone. *Something* apparently didn't want to be investigated or captured on film.

"They don't want us to record them," stated Mark. He was not a happy camper. He thought he captured compelling evidence but that was now gone.

"Do you know who it is, Laurie? Who is the evil guy in the basement?" I asked her.

She was hesitant and reluctant to reveal this to me. "I'm sorry I have to tell you this... but... it's his father, Mr. Jaeger.

The hairs stood up the back of my neck. I was speechless. *Mr. Jaeger. Here?*

"He wants Chris out of the house and Anita, he wants *you* all to himself."

Laurie said she couldn't stay any longer. She felt drained and ill, and her team packed up.

After they left Chris turned to me and said, "Don't worry Mom, I'm not going anywhere."

II.

Fragments of Souls
Summer of 2010

"Rummaging in our souls, we often dig up something that ought to have lain there unnoticed."

-Leo Tolstoy, Anna Karenina

CHAPTER 14
PARANORMAL PANDEMONIUM

The word pandemonium was coined by Milton in his 1667 Paradise Lost: "*A solemn Councel forthwith to be held At Pandæmonium, the high Capital of Satan and his Peers.*"

To get the word, Milton combined a couple of Greek roots, pan meaning all and demon, with the Latin-*ium* ending. So pandemonium is literally the place of all demons. Within a century or so, the word was being used to describe things akin to a real hell and eventually to the modern meaning of confusion, tumult, or uproar. *(Source: http://www.wordorigins.org/index.php/site/pandemonium/)*

This perfectly described the situation we were now facing in my home.

The month of May 2010 started with poltergeist activity that included not only what Chris and I were experiencing but Chris' girlfriend Heather was feeling something was following her home after leaving our house as well.

On May 11, Chris walked into the kitchen after coming in late from his date and walked into a wall of cobwebs. He tried to wipe them off his face with his hands but they evaporated. Entering his room to get ready for bed he heard and saw a penny thrown against the door. Within several minutes, Heather texted him on his cell phone that while she was driving on her way home that she felt cobwebs in her car and that a penny had hit her leg.

A few days later, Chris once again came home from his date and as he went through the studio to use the downstairs bathroom he found that the drawers to my desk were all pulled out at the same equal distance. When he asked me the next morning if I heard anything that night like the sound of the drawers being opened, I said no. What was strange is the drawers do not open easily and when I open them, they make squeaking noises.

On the 13th, Chris and I were in the living room watching a video tape session from our camcorder that I was using for reference for one of the chapters in my book *Estate of Horror.* While watching the tape on the TV we started feeling cold drafts, and then several papers and a pen flew across the room. A plastic ice tea scoop flew out of the kitchen followed by a pair of Chris' slippers thrown from upstairs in the front hall. This never happened before when we reviewing Paul's tapes.

About two weeks later, it was time for the spirits to once again show themselves. It was May 26 and Chris was in the living room eating a snack. He was finishing some peanut butter from a jar and its red lid was on the TV table next to him.

SWOOSH!

"Mom did you just see that?"

The red lid had flown through the air and landed on top of the love seat. We were at a loss for words.

Later that evening, Heather, her cousin and her friend were at our house as they planned to go out that night. Heather went upstairs to fix her hair and I sat conversing with the girls.

Heather's cousin turned to me and asked, "Do you have a cat?"

When I answered no, she told me she heard a meow.

Shortly after, she said that Chris received a frantic text message from Heather upstairs. She was asking for help as she was stuck in the bathroom and the door would not open. She explained she heard a cat scratching outside of the door. She was very afraid and Chris ran upstairs to the rescue.

Meanwhile her cousin and her friend just sat on the love seat and were afraid to move.

"What is going here?" the girls asked.

I cautiously explained what had happened to me over the past year at my friend's house and they looked scared. Chris and Heather came downstairs, where Heather gathered her stuff and she and the girls left as quickly as possible. It seemed any new person entering my house had to be initiated to its idiosyncrasies. I was left wondering if the cat's spirit was of Paul's deceased cat Heidi and had it now taken up residence as our ghostly pet. Or, was it something imitating a cat?

We finished the month of May with some more activity – cold drafts wafting through the house with no source and money being thrown in various rooms – and we hoped that was it. But, of course, we were wrong. Based on all that had happened before, we should have known better!

On June 6, my elderly parents came to my house for the day due to their losing power at their house and it was too hot for them to stay there. Chris and I were cleaning up the dinner dishes and I mentioned that the kitchen looked a mess. Chris laughed and said my kitchen could never be as messy as Paul's kitchen. I opened the refrigerator to put something away and I felt something hit me on the shoulder. I looked down at the kitchen floor and it was a plastic ice tea scoop.

"Hey, what's the big idea, Chris?"

"I didn't do anything!"

As Chris said that, a penny flew off the microwave oven, landing between my legs, and started spinning on the floor. By that time, my parents got up from the table to see what was going on in the kitchen. As they stood there in the doorway, a fork flipped out of the sink and landed on the counter. My parents were dumbfounded as they had heard all of our stories but had never seen anything like it before with their own eyes. Now they understood a little of what we had gone through at Paul's house.

On June 16, we had a contractor at the house working on new siding. After the first day of work, the contractor asked if he and his workers could leave their tools and equipment in the upstairs attic. I told them they could and secured the door that night.

The next day the contractor was walking around the back yard and handed me a brass candle snuffer that he found on the lawn near the attic steps.

"Here Anita, I wouldn't want this to get run over by a lawn mower."

I thanked him and took a good look at it. It was a candle snuffer from Paul's house. I had no idea how it got out of the attic as I remembered it was packed in a box placed up there.

The next two weeks would be fun and games for the ghosts as they took their activity outdoors now to torment our poor workers.

As the contractors removed the old siding on the second floor of my house, their tools would fly out of their belts and would fall down into the weeds below.

When the contractor was trying to fix the connection to my lamppost, he found pieces were missing. That wasn't so surprising – parts go missing on things all the time. It was the fact that these same parts reappeared twenty minutes later that stunned him.

Another day he reported that the garage door was going up and down by itself.

As the job neared completion they asked me what was going on with my house. Almost reluctantly, I confessed to them that my house seemed to be haunted. I shouldn't have been worried as to what their reaction would be because they said they had worked on old houses before and had some strange experiences themselves.

On the last day the workers were at my house, they needed to finish painting a small area near the garage. I went to the basement remembering that I had some paint they could use to prime the woodwork. I moved some of Paul's boxes out of the way to reach the can from a shelf.

"What the hell," Chris yelled from upstairs. "Mom, something just got thrown in the dining room!"

I quickly grabbed the paint and ran upstairs and as I entered the dining room, a sand block flew out of my studio and landed on the rug.

Chris held up a sharp awl that had been the first object out of my studio.

The workers came into the breezeway, between the garage and kitchen, wanting to know what was going on. Almost on cue, a large orange sponge came out of the sink, flew through the air over their heads, and landed at their feet. We started laughing at this absurd spectacle and one of the workers asked excitedly if he could take a few pictures inside, as he was a big fan of ghost hunting shows.

He wasn't even in the house a minute when suddenly he came running out of the house and said, "Forget the pictures!" It seems a pot lid from the drain board hit him squarely on the back as he was walking through the kitchen towards the dining room. The lid was still spinning on the floor as we looked past him. He did not go back in the house; he wasn't welcome.

As they finished packing up, one of the workers matter-of-factly turned to me and said, "I don't know if you know this but your house has been known in the township as always being haunted.

"What are you talking about?" I asked, surprised.

"I mentioned to my father what house I was working on and the street address and he said, when he was growing up this property was vacant for a long time and people would walk by quickly and not linger near the grounds."

He had more. "Teens would go in the back of the secluded property and have drinking parties. When the neighbors would call the police, the kids would run and disappear down a manhole that connects to old tunnels used during the Civil War and come out of the sewers several blocks away."

I was very intrigued. I had heard from an elderly neighbor that the area had a lot of history and that some of the tunnels' entrances were located in the back of my property but had been sealed over years ago by the township.

"Really? That was a dangerous thing to do as those tunnels could have collapsed on them," I exclaimed.

"Yeah, the crazy kids took big risks because the police could never catch them. They would tease each other and had a saying that, 'if the police didn't catch you the ghosts would!'"

CHAPTER 15

RELUCTANT PSYCHIC

June of 2010 was a big month for the dead coming to Chris. Yes, you read that right. Let me explain.

One morning Chris handed me a note that he wrote down from his dream that night and asked me to look up someone's name.

I looked at it. Written on the paper was the name Martin Sandberger with the numbers 3, 30, and 98.

"Who's this, Chris?"

"I don't know, some old guy told me he worked with Paul's father." That was all Chris said.

I did not look up the name and forgot about it, as I was busy with the frantic pace of working on my client's projects, taking care of the house, looking after my sick parents at their house and trying to write the next chapter for my *Estate of Horror* manuscript.

A week went by before Chris asked me again if I had looked up the name. I had to admit to Chris I was not familiar with searching on Google so Chris finally looked up the name on Wikipedia and found some startling facts on this person who, we found, was recently deceased.

"Ahhh Mom, you are not going to believe this!" Chris was stunned and said he had the chills when he began to read the information:

> Martin Sandberger, German Nazi died 3/30 of this year 2010 at the age of 98 (born August 17, 1911) and was a member of Schutz staffel SD. SS Colonel Commander of group in Estonia and the Baltic states responsible for the mass murder of civilians and Jews.

We could barely wrap our heads around this information. It made Chris and I uncomfortable and unsettled to have such an evil and violent personage visit him in his dreams and from so long ago.

It was only a few days later, on June 28, that Chris had another disturbing visit, and wrote this in his bedside diary: "Hanz Joanhim Seyering, 30116, Waffel 33-45 Father and Medicine, 900." When we looked it up on the internet, we found that Chris was off by one letter in the name he'd written for this actual person, but that what he dreamt was disconcerting:

> Hans Joachim Sewering, born on 30-1-16 (German style of writing birth dates compared to our date writing of January 30, 1916). Died June 18, 2010 at age 94. He was a German Physician in the Waffen SS in WWII and a member from 1933-1945. Sewering was a doctor at a death camp and responsible for the death/murder of 900 handicap children.

There was the word *father* Chris wrote along with the other information. Did Sewering have a connection to Paul's father too?

I wrote a frantic e-mail to Laurie Hull on June 28, 2010

Dear Laurie -

Chris has been receiving messages from recently dead Nazi SS people! He wrote down several names in the last few weeks with numbers and dates. After several sleepless nights, he looked these names up on Wikipedia and our blood went cold! The two men that visited Chris have just died recently and they were members of the Nazi SS elite force responsible for the deaths of over 1000 people! Chris is a wreck! Do you think it would help him to talk to Randy since Randy knows first-hand about being a medium? Could you offer Chris any advice? You have been dealing with dead people for most of your life. How do you do it? My son is afraid to open himself up to more because he does not know what will happen. Can you please help! Thanks, Anita

CHAPTER 16
CHRIS WAS REICH?

One of the most unbelievable dreams Chris ever dictated to me was on the morning of June 29, 2010. He called me into his bedroom that morning around 8:00 a.m. when he heard me up and moving around. I knew something was not right when I heard the sound of his tired voice. I found him lying face down on his pillow and he seemed to be racking his brain to make an orderly sense of the images and information he received during the night. He told me to grab a paper and pen to write the things he was going to dictate to me.

"I am just going to talk, mom and just write down whatever I say. Don't stop me unless I stop otherwise I may lose my train of thought."

I sat down on the edge of his bed and felt I could hardly breathe, as I knew what he was to going to reveal to me would be extraordinary.

"Go ahead, Chris."

"There are multiple things and they happened all at once. There is this dude sitting at his desk writing something and his name is Rumbell or Rumbol; I think that's how it is spelled. He is writing at his desk and behind him is a lady who is behind prison bars in a cell and she is wearing a white prom dress and waving a dead flower. I can see that above her, there are initials scratched on the concrete wall of the cell and the initials are M L J. She has this ball made of clear glass next to her foot with the number 6 on it painted in red."

Chris paused. "I see the guy, you know, the actor who played the sadistic Nazi in the movie, *Inglorious Bastards.* I think his name is Christof Waltz? So I picked up the name of Christof with the last name Probe…I get the word Probastos?"

Chris seemed confused with this name as he thought it meant some kind of ape. "Or is it proboscis? Isn't that an elephant's trunk?" he asked me.

"Honey, I'm not sure. Go on."

"There is another guy named Hans holding up a paper with the date 1943. I came up with these other names of Hans and De Graf, and then last names I can't fully pronounce. All three men are somehow related. There is a guy's name Schillerberg. Then Schetsfallal or Schiten struffel. I don't know - I can't speak German!" Chris blurted out in exasperation.

"The lady in prison says to someone in the shadows, 'Shame on you (for your scheme or something like that)' and is pointing her finger at them. They reply to her, 'Well, screw you, we'll take care of you.'"

He continued as I wrote down more of the dream.

"I am seeing all these people and Hans and Christof are in the background with shadows, and the woman, the one in the prison cell, is coming forward. She tells me 'Hello.' The clear ball is still near her but the number 6 is now dripping blood. Hans looks at her as she turns around with a black square box that has turrets on the top-like a castle or chess piece. Looks like a rook?"

Chris again took a moment to gather his thoughts.

"Then there is another different scene. There is another Hans, different from the others, who is talking to someone named Heidi, telling her to 'take your place' as she is an actress and acting in a play. Then a man calls out, "Act 1, Scene 2" and claps one of those scene boards together."

"Going back, there are others near the woman in prison. They look at each other and then me and start talking real fast with agitation. Before something happens to them they yell something like 'Let__ Fre_ liv__!' But I can't understand them, and I got so frightened and I woke up!"

Chris raised his head from the pillow and said he felt drained and had a massive headache. He would find it tough to function the rest of the day as the dream took so much out of him.

I made some breakfast hoping it would make Chris feel better. We quickly ate and directly went to the computer to search for his mysterious dream visitors. It did not take us long to find information on the website for the United Kingdom's newspaper, The Guardian, that lists recently deceased celebrities in Europe.

We believed that we found them.

Fred Rombell (Chris was off by one letter) was a German writer who was born in 1941 and died on June 22, 2010 at the age of 69.

The lady wearing white and holding the dead flower behind prison bars, with the initials MLJ, was for Mary Louise Jahn, who also died June 22, 2010 at the age of 92.

Mary Louise Jahn was a member of the White Rose, an underground organization of university students that protested against the brutality of the Third Reich and would print out pamphlets and distribute them voicing for freedom against this regime. The Gestapo imprisoned her in 1943 along with the six core members of the group at Stadelheim Prison. Three of the members - Hans Scholl, his sister Sophia Scholl, and Christoph Probst - were all executed by decapitation on February 22, 1943.

The last thing that Hans Scholl yelled out before being executed was "LET FREEDOM LIVE!"

Later, group members Willi Graf and Alex Schmorell were executed on July 13, 1943 and Professor Kurt Huber executed October 13, 1943.

All were decapitated by the Schutzstaffel, known to most people as the SS; the same organization that I was told Paul's father was affiliated with. Walter Schellenberg was commander of the SD (division of Gestapo) at that time. Another division of the Gestapo, called Abwehr, dealt with counter intelligence and rooted out enemies of the state. After Hitler dismantled the Abwehr after a failed coup in 1944, Walter Schellenberg became head of all secret services. One of his attack units murdered over 633,000 civilians on March 30, 1943.

Other people who had showed up in Chris' dream were Heidi Kabel, an actress in Germany who died on June 15, 2010 at the age of 92 and her husband Hans who directed her in "low" plays. "Low German" or "Low Saxon" is a West Germanic language spoken mainly in northern Germany and the eastern part of the Netherlands. It is descended from Old Saxon in its earliest form.

What I find fantastic about this particular dream is the relationship these ghosts present. At first they seem random and not connected but then realizing they were all German personalities and historical figures, and although did not all live in the time frame they all died within a week of each other! It is as if the ghosts piggybacked on the same ether plane ride to contact Chris because of the coincidence of the time of their deaths. The fact remained that they appeared after Laurie told us that Paul's father was in the basement and there was other evil there. Perhaps they contacted Chris because he was open and receptive, having been approached in dreams before. Now Chris seemed to be a conduit for much of the paranormal activity.

CHAPTER 17
THE SHADOW MAN

Chris awoke suddenly around 6 a.m. and as his eyes adjusted to the dim light in his room he saw a figure near his lounge chair. He had the presence of mind to grab his phone and quickly snapped a picture with its camera before going back to sleep. When he woke up several hours later, he thought he had dreamed the event. That was until he looked at the strange and frightening image he had actually captured

He showed the photo to me and I could not find words, There, hovering above a box of books on the bedroom floor, was what looked like a black-cloaked, hooded creature. It seemed to be floating off the floor near the bottom of his bed. The object was so dense that you couldn't see through it or see Chris' Phillies shirt that was draped over the top of the chair.

"THAT was in your room this morning? Are you OK?"

"Well, I was scared shitless when I saw it and all I could think was to grab my phone that was near me and snap a photo. I wasn't even sure this morning the whole episode was real but here you have it. I caught "it" on my cell phone."

I suggested he take another photo of the chair to compare before and after shots. In the frames, there is a slight change of the shirts moved before Chris took his other photo but both photos were taken the same morning.

This was not our first experience with the entities that some people call shadow people. Less than a year before, in August 2009, our cousins had visited Paul's house as Chris and I continued the cleanup there, hoping to capture some paranormal activity on their cameras. One of our cousins, Karen, sat on a chair in the basement and soon felt a presence behind her. She quickly snapped a photo behind her and we saw that she had captured the image of a distinct figure against the stark, blank wall. It looked like it was wearing a brimmed hat, like a Derby.

When she had showed me the image back then I had chills down my spine.

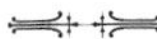

Chris and I had also seen unexplained shadows darting along the baseboards and ceilings in our home starting on that terrifying Christmas Eve in December 2009, and it seemed to be happening more frequently. These shadows seemed to accompany poltergeist activity at the same time. I began to explore further this phenomenon of shadow people in online postings and reports from witnesses on paranormal community websites.

A shadow person–said to be a paranormal entity-can appear as a tall or thin black silhouette or even manifest itself as a black mass. Their movement is described as being very quick and disjointed and at times they seem to "hop" to another part of a surrounding. I witnessed this type of movement on that Christmas Eve day when the shadow-being darted into the bathroom after Chris and then threw his shaver into the hallway. Then, just as quickly "it" danced down the stairs to the first floor and completely disappeared.

These shadow figures are also known as the Hat-Man, who wears a "Zorro-type" hat or "Fedora or Derby type" hat." He might wear a suit and a cape or a long trench coat, and can possess glowing red eyes. Even more terrifying is an entity reported covered in a hooded black cloak with no feet!

One theory is that shadow people are psychological in nature, and somehow linked to a stressful lifestyle. I had to admit my son and me, and my brother and his family, were living with great stressors. I was taking care of my elderly parents' day-to-day health care needs with no end in sight. My dad's Parkinson's disease was progressing and making his daily functions very difficult, and my mom's constant visits to the emergency room following a heart attack keep us in a constant state of crisis. The regime of medications she was taking wreaked havoc with her delicate system. She was falling frequently and my dad worried more about her than himself. I hated to call my poor brother in the morning when the next incident occurred with them. Instead of giving him a pleasant, "Good morning, how are you?" I'd have to break the bad news of "mom is in the hospital again." We were all so weary and worried.

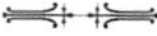

A strange man came to Chris in a dream one night in July and told him he was very angry that the neighbor's dogs, which lived next door, were "pipsqueaks" and wanted them to stop barking at his "beauty," a big, black "wolf dog" with red glowing eyes. Chris could see that the figure was wearing farmers' overalls that were covered in dirt, and a brimmed hat, and could see that the man had the dog tied up in our backyard but the yard looked different. Chris felt he was viewing a scene from the past - possibly from the early 1900's - and the man was definitely not from our time.

Coincidentally, I caught a good look at a "shadow man" one evening while sitting in my lounge chair opposite the front hallway of my house and watching TV. Out of the corner of my left eye I saw him. A tall dark figure, at least seven feet tall, wearing a brimmed hat. I was so shocked I just froze in my chair. It seemed to linger a few seconds and I finally mustered up the courage and said in a firm voice, "Hey, I'm minding my own business here, don't bother me!" The figure just continued to "walk" to the front door and then vanished through the solid door. I blinked once or twice and started to question myself. Did I just see that? I had to grapple with the answer. I was so stunned. I knew what I saw was not a hallucination or optical illusion. It was very real!

This was something new. We had never experienced or seen anything like this before in my house, only at Paul's. The dark presence had not shown aggression towards me. Maybe I was just witnessing part of my home's original history and the shadow man was an echo of a spirit or ghost of someone who had existed here long ago.

One morning, a week later, Chris displayed a very disturbed demeanor. He told me the strange man with the brimmed hat, whom Chris now called the "Hat Man," came to him again and wanted him to know "Oatman MINE." Chris also recalled something about the desert and the west but had no idea what that meant so he immediately googled the name Oatman on his cell phone and relayed the information to me as he sat on his bed.

"Hey Mom, I found someone named Oatman. There was a woman named Olive Oatman; she was only fourteen years old when she was crossing the Arizona desert with her pioneer Mormon family in 1851 and they were attacked by Apache Indians. Except for her and her sister, the whole family was massacred. She and her sister were captured and enslaved by the Indians. Later, Olive and her sister were sold to the Mojave Indians where they received blue chin tattoos by the tribe as symbols of their captivity and later to identify them as members of the tribe. Five years later, she was rescued (her sister had died of starvation) by white men and taken back to her brother, who had survived after being left for dead. Olive Oatman spent the rest of her life traveling and telling her incredible story on a lecture circuit and it became a popular subject of plays, novels, and poetry. She died of a heart attack in in 1903. Look, here's a picture of her and she still has the tattoo on her chin!"

I looked at the cell phone screen. It was a weird coincidence that Chris had this dream about the same time we started to watch the TV show *Hell on Wheels*. What caught my interest in the show was the actress who played a former brothel worker and was an outcast member of society due to her tattooed chin as a reminder of her early days as a captive of the Apache Indians.

I told Chris that this character in the show was based in on a real person. I had remembered reading one of my western history books and seeing a photo of a woman just like that with a tattooed chin. I didn't recall her name at the time, but now I realized it was Olive Oatman and her markings were exactly like the one the TV actress had on the show. What did the shadow man mean by saying, "Oatman MINE?" These people died over a hundred and fifty years ago. Did this shadow figure have some type of power over their spirits?

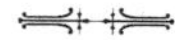

July wasn't going to end without further incident. The "Hat Man" was back; he once again came to Chris in a dream and it was more vivid this time.

I heard Chris yelling out in his sleep on the night of the 29th and ran into his room. He sat up startled and in a cold sweat. He told me that the shadow man revealed more about himself to him.

Chris saw him in our backyard again, wearing the same farmer's overalls and brimmed hat, and he had a companion - the large black dog with red eyes - with him. Chris told the man that he was trespassing on our property. The man looked up at him with sunken dark eyes and said, "I used to live here before I went to jail for committing murder." The dog started to bark at Chris with such ferocity that he was frightened and he forced himself to wake up.

But had he really awakened? As Chris' eyes tried to adjust to his dark bedroom he was suddenly aware that the "Hat Man' was at the bottom of his bed. And he wasn't alone! The big, black wolf dog was barking wildly at Chris, with the man holding tight to the leash. It's as if the dog wanted to tear Chris apart. The dog was so close that Chris could feel his hot, stinky breath.

Suddenly Chris was jolted awakened again, this time with me running into his room calling out, "Chris, are you alright?"

I quickly turned on the light and instinctively looked around the bedroom. I could see beads of sweat on his forehead.

"Huh? Oh, my God. I just had the most horrible dream!" He put his hands to his face.

I looked around the room and noticed a black spot on the carpet.

"What the hell is this?" I bent over and picked up what looked like a clump of long, black hair from an animal. "Where did this come from?"

Chris was now in a cold sweat and was shaking his head. "I don't know. Maybe it came from the dog?"

"What dog?"

I stood in the room dumbfounded as Chris explained what happened in his dream.

When he finished I said, "We have to get to the bottom of this! Tomorrow I am going to search county records and see what I can find out about the former owners of this property."

As I turned to leave his room I looked down at my hand and saw that the "ghost dog" hair had vanished!

I was now going into detective mode and this approach helped me to remain focused although I was terrified for us. Whatever was haunting our house I wanted to stand firm and not feed into fear. This was my house and no one or thing was going to make me afraid to live here.

The next day I spent several hours on our Delaware County Historical Society website. When I hit a dead end, I spent additional hours looking up old courthouse records. Then by chance one afternoon, remembering the child in Chris' dream, I began looking through orphan court records from the 1800's, and saw the names of several children recorded who had lived on our property. Could one of the children named in the records have been the frightened child Chris saw in one of his dreams? Then I went through old newspaper clippings on microfilm that dated from the early 1900's. I started reading articles about some of the local news in the county when I came across something about a farmer who went to jail for a most heinous crime. I then printed out the small article.

I couldn't wait to show the news article to Chris when he got home from work.

"Here, take a look at this!" I handed him the print out. "I think I know who that man is that is visiting in your dreams. His name was John Stanton and he went to prison in the early 1900's for murdering his wife!"

CHAPTER 18
BENJAMIN FOSTER

After new siding had been installed on my house, Chris and I decided we needed to paint the attic door and window on my garage as these now looked decidedly shabby. It was mid-July and it was a pleasant, warm day and not very humid, great factors for drying outdoor paint. I had been mixing the separate cans of black and white paint on the attic door landing, and Chris went to retrieve the can of black paint. When he saw black paint dripping on the new railing, he yelled, calling me out as being sloppy.

"I didn't do that," I answered indignantly.

We saw that my paint stick was still in the paint can but blobs of black paint were splashed all over the drop cloth as well as the railing

"Huh? Who did that?" asked Chris.

"It's like some little kid playing and having fun with the paint stick at our expense," I stated.

We stood there for another minute and then Chris decided to work on the black part of the window trim that was an X design. Against the white background the X made the attic door look like a barn loft door.

A short time later, he came over to me, put down his paint brush and grabbed the white paint and a new brush to finish the job. He walked over to the freshly painted black X on the door and yelled, "WHAT THE HELL?"

The white areas of the door had been marked with wet black paint! It looked like a small child's handprint on the white of the door, and on another part of the door appeared words. To us it looked like the word HELP, followed by either LAGOS or LOGOS.

We wondered what was responsible for this new activity and even considered that it might be a new one. We'd been experiencing an increase in mischievous activity and this one felt playful compared to others. Viewing the painted handprint and writing on the garage door, they seemed to come from a child.

The next morning Chris came to me with the answer. The ghost of a child had visited him. Benjamin Foster was his name and his family's farm had been down our street in the early 1800's on what is now known as the Foster Track Tot Lot.

Among the messages the little boy gave Chris was that the number 8 was significant; that is how old he was when he died. Chris felt that he died on or around our property. Chris also received a date of 1757 as part of the message. Although Benjamin has been here as a spirit for a very long time, over a hundred years or more, we could not determine if the 1757 is related to the young boy, as we can't find any records on him.

Benjamin told Chris that it was his handprint and he needed our help. He said he was risking being hurt by the "bad man" by telling us what was going on here. We were not sure if the "bad man" was Paul's father or something else, as Benjamin did not specify. He said that there was a very evil entity that took different forms, like a shape shifter. It could even be in the form of a bent, cloaked dark figure like the one Chris captured on his cell phone that one morning.

Feeling helpless, Chris and I were not sure if we were able to do anything.

Benjamin was upset with the situation that the evil thing was now here. Benjamin said the evil one's nickname is "Dolce con el Diablo" (dessert with the Devil). Chris drew me a picture and it was a depiction of a very nasty, shrouded-looking thing with razor sharp teeth. Chris said it preys on the fears of the other spirits that are in our house. This thing is also present at times in our upstairs bathroom!

Benjamin also apologized for having cut us and said he had to do this on "Dolce con el Diablo's" orders or he will be punished. Indeed, Chris and I had been finding scratches on our legs and arms and weren't sure where they were coming from. I'd had a terrifying incident of being scratched while in our upstairs bathroom shower. I had felt a searing, sharp, burning pain suddenly on my chest. I quickly got out of the shower and saw, to my horror, three long scratches that drew blood going across my chest. The scratches took a week to heal. Was this Benjamin's doing or was this something evil disguising itself and letting Benjamin take the blame?

The little boy said he loved to be around Chris for protection, that he likes to be in Chris' room as he is afraid of what he calls the "bad man in the basement." He also said he loved his room with all the toys. He plays with the movie monster and action figure collectibles and that is why Chris finds things often moved around in the room. But when he feels Chris is ignoring him, Benjamin seems to have a "temper tantrum," as Chris had found some figures tossed around the room and broken. This has made Chris feel both angry and upset but he also felt sorry for this little child.

Could this be the child mentioned on the EVP Laurie Hull had picked up in our basement with her equipment way back in January 2010, when she asked who was the oldest here on my property and we heard it was "the boy first." I contacted Laurie again to let her know of this new turn and she said she and her team would come to the house.

⁂

It was shortly after, that Laurie came to see the garage. She agreed that she also picked up the number 8 and it was associated with a child and the word looked like either "Help" or "Lagos." Laurie wasn't familiar with the word Lagos but later researched indicated that this could possibly be Latin for LORD.

As always, it is so good to have Laurie's feedback at the house. Chris and I agreed with Laurie that we need focused guidelines for a more controlled investigation in the future. We knew that what we saw and experienced, and were still experiencing, had been validated by Laurie's investigative team. Their findings were in the report she now handed to me. On an Excel spreadsheet she had one of her team members fill out the list of unexplainable incidents they experienced in our house. The report also included a CD of the EVPs she had captured on her digital device that night in April. The report concluded that our house was a unique situation and had all the necessary elements present that are in a haunting.

They were giving us full support and assistance, and we were looking forward to when she could coordinate another investigation. But in the following weeks Laurie and her team were busy with other investigations and helping others deal with their own hauntings. Laurie admitted to me that years earlier when she started her group of paranormal investigators it was usual to get only four calls a month to look into a "haunting situation." Now in a climate of more people believing in the paranormal and the acceptance of it being a popular subject of conversation, and the proliferation of paranormal TV shows, books and movies, Laurie's group was getting hundreds of calls a month to investigate cases of the supernatural.

In August, she called me and admitted to me that there may be nothing more she or her team could do for us. She told me something she had not mentioned before but felt it could have some bearing on the continued haunting situation involving Paul and his family.

"Anita," Laurie said, "I do believe there was a curse placed on your friend's family years ago and that there is a dangerous dark entity that is strongly attached now to your house and property. Frankly, we are not equipped to handle this."

"What are we talking about Laurie?"

"I think it would be best that you look into someone who could bless and confront this entity and perform an exorcism your house."

When I hung up the phone all I could think was, *Jesus, how much worse can it get?*

III.

Realm of Spirits
2011-2013

Houses are not haunted. We are haunted, and regardless of the architecture with which we surround ourselves, our ghosts stay with us until we ourselves are ghosts.

-Dean Koontz, Velocity

CHAPTER 19
A PRESENCE AND PRESENTS

Most of our paranormal experiences in the house made us feel we were at odds with some malevolent force but something happened in early 2010 that would make us believe we were dealing with something entirely different and of a benevolent nature.

One evening Chris' found several strands of fine blue threads on his art table that was set up in our living room. At first, he thought I had left them as I sometimes do handwork nearby. However, these were not mine, as I didn't recall having threads like these in my sewing box. They were raw, unrefined, and looked like silk.

I didn't throw them away but placed them on our coffee table and the next morning I found the threads on our dark carpet. I was astounded. They had been turned into a work of art! What had been only a few hours before just plain threads had now been worked into an intricate looped pattern. We thought this incredible and had no explanation. Something or *someone* had gone through a great deal of trouble to make this. I carefully placed them in an envelope for safekeeping. I showed it to my mom and another friend of hers and they were equally mystified on how it was done. It was like a crocheting technique but much finer, more like tatting.

I had heard of people receiving unusual gifts that they felt were left from deceased loved ones. A childhood friend had told me of dimes that showed up at her brother's new dental office and they felt it was their deceased father showing them his approval for his son's new venture. Indeed, they have a whole jar of them now.

Besides coins I've heard of white feathers appearing out of thin air in order to grab a loved one's attention. A dear friend of our family told us years ago that after the premature death of her granddaughter's husband they started finding feathers left throughout the house. It just wasn't a random feather here and there. They actually collected a vase full of white feathers! They were convinced that his spirit was there in visitation to let them know he was okay and he was leaving them as a loving reminder to his wife and children that he was watching over them. This gave them comfort in the midst of their grief.

But I had never been the recipient of this incredible phenomenon. Until now.

I wasn't aware this type of phenomena even had a name --an apport. It means a physical object which has been paranormally transported into a closed space or container, suggesting the passage of "matter through matter." (*Source: Historical Terms Glossary of the Parapsychological Association)*

Is that what I was finding?

A year later, in 2011, I received two more thread pieces within several days of each other. As before, they were blue and the threads were of a type I do not own or have in the house, although I use vintage threads to sew my doll outfits.

These were even more elaborate than the first. They appeared suddenly out of nowhere, in the living room. I had just walked through that room to the kitchen and when I came back, only a minute later, there they were on the rug.

Several days later while I was sweeping my stairs, I saw another piece appear before me on a step. I didn't know what they meant and who or what was leaving these for me to find.

I felt I was dealing with a feminine spirit that was interacting with me. There seemed an air of kindness and a gentle, motherly concern that I was picking up psychically along with the gifts she was leaving. The upstairs bathroom was the very first place we were made aware, by Laurie Hull and the all-female psychic team who had visited in September of 2011, that there was indeed a lady spirit present in the house, whose old fashioned perfume of roses and lavender we smelled.

Laurie got the name Marjorie and believed that she was an older lady, a caregiver or nanny from the Victorian period.

An apparition of an older woman was sighted at my front door only two hours before Laurie and her team came to my house. It was 10 a.m. on that Sunday morning and my mom's daytime caregiver was driving by my house. As she looked at my house, she saw an older woman standing just inside the door. She appeared to be wearing an old-fashioned high neck blouse, with her graying hair swept up in a Gibson Girl style top knot. The poor woman was so startled she almost drove her car off the road!

When, a few days later, she reported to me what she had seen, I investigated and found that there is only eight inches of space between my front storm door and the solid wood door and that is not enough room for any adult human body to fit. I was feeling vindicated that indeed there was a protective female presence in my house and her name was Marjorie.

I did not receive any more gifts of ghost threads the whole year of 2012 and figured that was the end of that. However in February of 2013, I again found a threaded piece in the upstairs bathroom, on the window sill and it was red! Chris had clipped a long piece of red thread from his new T-shirt and threw it into the trashcan on Sunday night. By Wednesday morning, I found the thread on the floor, with a pattern worked into it.

Two weeks later, on a Sunday evening, Chris called me at my mother's house to tell me that I had another gift left in the upstairs bathroom. This time it was purple and gray threads.

On March 25, 2013, Palm Sunday, I got a surprise under my pajamas that sat on top of my bed. I showed a photo of it to my literary agent who emailed me back and said she thought she saw a child's face in the threads. Could the threads have a ghostly message in them or were we experiencing pareidolia? (This is described as a psychological phenomenon that involves a stimulus wherein the mind perceives familiar patterns of something where none exists).

In April, a few weeks later on another Sunday, Chris called me once again to let me know a gift was left on my steps, much like two years before. This time the thread color was black and the design was like an eternity knot.

August arrived and with it came the most elaborate gift I've received, found outside my breezeway door. I hadn't received any threads for several months and was surprised and startled to see how long this piece was. The pieces in the past had been several inches in length and very delicate. This one, made of a heavier silky type thread, was 12 inches long!

In 2014, the threads began to appear outside of my home. In June, Chris received a gift of brown "ghost" threads on his bedroom floor and he lived three blocks away.

On September 30, he found a blue thread on the back of my light green sweater while we were in a department store. They were not there a few moments earlier. We wondered if our ghost friend liked to travel, or whether she was attached to either Chris or I, or both of us.

The threads still appear from time to time. As late as April 2015, while I was at Chris' house, I was coming into the house from the outside patio and there, right on the welcome mat, was a turquoise threaded piece that was not there minutes ago. It was lovely and everyone was amazed over this newest work of art from beyond.

Whether "Marjorie" created the gifts from nothing or just manipulated an object into something else, it will always be a matter of debate. It is still an extraordinary thing to happen and I feel unbelievably privileged.

CHAPTER 20

A FINAL FLY OVER

One is never prepared to say goodbye to their parents. The death of both of your parents makes you an orphan and it is hard accepting that title. The one thing that has made my parents' parting tolerable was to know they are now together for eternity. That, and the knowledge I did all I could, with my brother and family, to give them their final wishes.

If any two people were destined to love in this world it would be Aurora Castellano and Vincent Intenzo. For you see, my dad was born in my mother's house!

In 1920, newlyweds Josephine and Anthony Intenzo rented a third floor apartment in a ten-room house that belonged to Donato and Philomena Castellano (my mom's family) at 16th and Ellsworth in South Philly. My dad was born on the third floor and eleven months later my mom was born on the second floor. The Intenzos moved away the following year and it wasn't until nineteen years later that my parents met again through mutual friends and then fell in love. After they married they wound up living in the same third floor apartment for five years. Together they built a life, family and business together and celebrated sixty-five years of marriage. My parents were truly destined to love!

My dad was the first to pass away at home on June 16, 2011, after suffering with Parkinson's disease for ten years. He took his diagnosis of Parkinson's with grace and dignity and never complained or bemoaned the fact that this terrible disease was inflicted upon him. He took his meds and was still able to drive, go into his place of business, do home projects and work on his art. Indeed, his neurologist has one of his fine pen and ink drawings displayed in his office.

When I was growing up, my dad seemed invincible and bigger than life. He was tall, handsome and all who knew him recognized a rare human being who was gifted with "golden hands," a caring heart and humane spirit. He was a proud man who shunned controversy, hated hypocrisy and lived within a moral and honest compass. I have no doubt at the moment my Dad was standing in front of Heaven's Pearly Gates he was scrutinizing them to see if they have been hung right and in proper alignment. That's how my dad was. He was always seeking perfection in an imperfect world.

I don't think my dad knew the full impact he had on people's lives as he himself was shy about praising himself because he was such a private and, at times, a solitary person. My dad wasn't a religious person; he preferred to keep his spiritual opinions to himself but he felt there was something good in all religions and kept an open mind. He was a deep thinker and had the heart of a poet and the soul of an artist. He loved the west and it influenced the many drawings and paintings that show the beautiful colorful and rugged landscapes of the area. He was an incredible draftsman, which was obvious from his detailed pencil, and pen and ink, drawings he has left behind. Some of his children and grandchildren carry on his wonderful artistic legacy today by pursuing careers in the art field.

When I think of my dad, I think of courage. He enlisted at the age of twenty-one when WW II broke out. He trained in the States to become a radio/radar man and was part of a ten member crew of a B-24 bomber that came together in Tucson, Arizona. They were shipped out to Europe as part of the 451st Bomb Group 49th Wing of the 15th Air Force that landed in France in January 1945. From there they went to Foggia, Italy and were encamped there and made their bombing raids from Italy over to Northern and Central Europe, the Po Valley and the Rhineland. Ironically, he was stationed right near where his father was born and raised before coming to America.

My dad and his crew flew over twenty-two missions during those last six months before the war ended in Europe. Each mission involved bombing key areas that supplied the German army and their allies. Planes were subject to dangerous conditions each time they went out on a mission, such as enemy fighter planes, cannons and rockets firing "flak" which were incendiary bombs that hung in the air and could damage or destroy a plane it came in contact with. It is a fact that over 80,000 airmen lost their lives in the European air campaign alone.

In April, 1945, while dropping bombs near Zagreb, Yugoslavia, my dad's plane was hit by enemy fire. The pilot, Gates Christensen, who became my dad's lifelong friend, asked the men if they wanted to bail out over enemy territory or stay with the plane and try to land it.

The crew chose to stay with the plane. They first dropped the rest of their payload of bombs and then crashed landed on the plane's belly, as their landing gear had been destroyed, in an open field in Yugoslavia. Luck was with them. They weren't seriously injured and they were found by Tito's allied underground and were kept safe until they were picked up and taken back to base. Their damaged plane was left behind, a grim reminder of one of the many fatalities of war.

When the war ended in Europe, the 451st Bomb Group was broken up and the men were headed home for good. Many went back to civilian life and tried to pick up the pieces of their lives that the war had interrupted. My dad, like so many of his fellow soldiers, was now mature beyond his years, tempered by what he had been through, disciplined by his military training and sacrifices. His group married in record numbers. My dad married the love of his life, his fiancée Aurora, on May 18th, 1946.

My father's last days weren't easy. Starting in late January 2011, he was rushed to the hospital with renal failure. After an emergency operation to unblock an artery in his kidney he still had to have a bladder tube inserted. Then then discovered he wasn't able to swallow solid food so he then had a feeding tube implanted. He suffered terrible pain but fought stubbornly a soldier's last stand against approaching death. Always in control, he found it hard to concede to the body's imperfection and the growing need to depend on others for support.

We brought him home from the hospital on hospice care, as we were told by the doctors there was nothing else they could do for him. Always the one in charge, my dad was now the charge of others. That was hard for him. The thing that bothered him the most was that he no longer could be the strong, capable man but had to now give over his frail body to me to help clean him up after an accident. He was mortified that his daughter had to do that. But I took it as my chance to do one last act of love for a man who had been a wonderful, kind and devoted father. He thanked me in a choked whisper.

The day my dad died I was sitting with him quietly, as my mother was taken for a doctor's appointment. I told him he could "go" as my mom would be taken care of. As I said this I saw a gold orb fly between us and then a dark shadow cross over his face. I knew "something" was here to take him through the veil.

Only days before, my mom's night caregivers and I had heard the sounds of knocking on our front door but no one was there. We heard the sound of someone shuffling with a cane down the tiled hallway, just like my dad's father would do with his cane and who died in 1985.

That night, June 16, 2011, my father passed away in the arms of his beloved wife. He was laid to rest with a military honor guard and after taps was played, a large, lone wild butterfly suddenly appeared and circled his casket just once and then fluttered off to a where a statue of Jesus stood. It had been the practice of the airmen of my dad's B-24 bomber crew to do a "fly over" during war time for a fallen comrade. Imagine my surprise later hearing of the practice of releasing captured butterflies, as they are the symbol of resurrection, at a person's funeral and then actually witnessing the sudden appearance of the wild butterfly. It's as if the butterfly was doing this one last honor for my dad and his spirit was saying goodbye to us.

Several weeks later, on July 4, Chris, texted me that his grandfather had come to him in a dream, joined by his deceased sister Rachael. He asked Chris to relay to us that he was fine, and that his deceased father, his dear friend Mario and his brother-in-law Tom Masci, who had very a close birthday with my dad, were there to greet him and cross him over.

As Chris related to me, "Poppy says 'Hi.' He looked happy and healthy, like he did thirty years ago. He was wearing the blue sweater he was buried in. He came through to let us know he is OK and he has a warning for us and information on the object in the basement."

Chris first texted me, "Aunt Ray talked to the head of the Indian Spiritual Counsel and what we have in our house is a level 2, 3-way changers or thrillers as they call them over there."

Chris then sent his second text. Poppy says, "There is some shit going on right now (in the spirit world,) a real shake up on the other side, someone called the 'new blood' is causing problems and also he wishes everyone a happy 4th!"

I was not surprised by this message from my dad as I had asked him before he died to please watch out for us and help us. Had he heard me after all, even in his coma? Seems he did!

CHAPTER 21
BACKYARD GRAVEYARD

A person's bathroom should be a private place. My second floor bathroom has become something else entirely. To look at my bathroom it appears normal in every way. It's a modest size compared to today's more modern spacious bathrooms. No fancy Jacuzzi or soaking tub. It has been upgraded through the last seventy years with new tile, fixtures, wallpaper and curtains. I never gave this room a second thought that it could be anything else but what it is – a bathroom.

But it has evolved into something different over the last few years. It seems to be a place that attracts invisible entities that leave multiple hand and finger prints on my vanity mirror at different times. This is also where I have been attacked in the shower by vicious scratches across my chest by some dark energy. Psychic medium Laurie Hull received scratches on her arm here during her investigation in April 2010.

We have witnessed objects picked up and thrown from the bathroom into the hallway and down the stairs: Chris' shaver, my contact lens case, coins, keychains and a rubber door stop. This poltergeist activity only started after Paul died. I had never seen any of these things occur before his death. There seems to be a something - maybe a portal - on the back wall where I've seen fleeting thin shadows dart under the window frame, so evident against the white tiles, while I'm sitting on the throne. I should be able to relax here, have a private moment and not think twice that I could be harmed in my little sanctuary. There had to be an explanation why my bathroom has become a place of concern, conflict and supernatural activity.

The reason I believe there *is* a portal in our bathroom came about from several incidents and this time not directly connected to Paul's death but perhaps resulting from the energy transported with his items to my home; they activated areas that normally were not paranormally active before.

Chris had a dream in which a ghostly female caregiver held a small, golden haired child in her arms and the little girl was dead. Chris got the impression that the child's name was Rebecca and she was only four years old.

This lady's appearance to Chris as someone grieving the loss of the child in her arms appeared to have a message for him as she directed him to the bathroom window. She was very sad as she pointed to an area in our back yard as if to say that you could see the little girl's grave from there. Although this window is now in a bathroom, who knows what room our lady ghost thinks she is still in one hundred forty years ago. I'm sure ghosts don't think about time the way we do. They possibly don't realize the old farm house is long gone and it's now my Cape Cod built over top of that foundation.

Chris awoke crying as he later told me the little girl was so adorable at first but then she turned into a decaying skeleton! He was confused over this, as he had a dream a month earlier of a little boy in dirty overalls – also about 4 years old - and this child told him he was buried in the back yard. Chris saw the details of a disintegrated, old wooden cross that was no longer visible but buried now in the ground and underneath it the little boy was laid to rest with his toy wooden blocks and a favorite ball.

We wondered if we were supposed to find this grave and give the child a burial in a churchyard. A century ago it was customary for family members to be buried at times on their own properties outside the city's jurisdiction. In fact, our area is still zoned "country" and we have had neighbors keep animals like horses, pigs and chickens on their properties.

We called on Laurie Hull again to see if she could help us to explore the death of this child. She and two of her team members Joyce and Carol, who specialized in grave dowsing, brought their dowsing equipment one Sunday morning a few weeks later and proceeded to take turns walking around in the back yard with the special metal rods. They were not aware of the area that Chris had pointed out to me that had been shown to him in his dream that was about one hundred feet behind our front shed.

Each of the three women took her time to explore separately and on her own and did not tell the others of the area she felt the strongest impression that might hold a grave. After the last woman made her sweep of the backyard, they compared notes. Incredibly, they had all arrived at the same spot behind the front shed exactly where Chris had told me he thought was a grave. Indeed, there was a depression in the earth under a clump of trees. Laurie announced that there were possibly two graves at the site! Although this news verified Chris' premonition, there was no way I was going to disturb the area by digging. We had enough going on and knew better not to possibly disturb things further.

We took a break and as we were enjoying a snack Laurie and the women took a look at some of the first ghost threads I had told them about. They were fascinated when they saw them. As we continued to discuss how they were made, Laurie had a strange look come over her. She asked for permission to go to the upstairs bathroom as something was drawing her attention there. Curious, we followed her.

Laurie remembered being scratched in this bathroom. She immediately went to the window and asked me if I had a room freshener in there. No, I had nothing like that in this bathroom, although I had a vanilla scented candle in the downstairs one. Suddenly a heady perfume of old-fashioned tea roses and lilacs enveloped us. It filled the room. We all smelled it.

"There's a Victorian lady here, Anita, and she is a very caring soul." Laurie stated.

What was going on? Could this be the "caregiver" that Chris had dreamt of holding the little dead girl?

We walked down the stairs and the scent faded. We gathered in my studio to discuss the significance of what happened in the upstairs bathroom and suddenly the scent of roses and lilacs filled the room. We moved to the dining room and the same thing happened. The ghost was following us! Joyce seemed to be particularly connected to the lady as the scent would emanate from near her each time. The women were ecstatic to have this shared paranormal experience.

But the next paranormal experience the woman encountered was not so pleasant. Laurie's companions wanted to see my infamous basement she had told them about. Since they were new to Laurie's team I warned them that we could be in for some unexpected confrontations. It was that unpredictable.

Carol was the first to say something as she made her way to the back wall of the basement where Laurie had felt the threatening presence of a dark spirit.

"I think you have more than one really bad thing here, Anita." She paused a moment, looking around. "What's with the uniformed soldiers?"

I wasn't sure what era she was talking about, given the long history of my property dating back to before the Civil War.

"Oh my God!" Carol's eyes grew wide. "They're Nazis! You have three Nazi SS officers here... in your basement, Anita!"

Joyce followed Carol's incredible statement with a sudden outburst. "OW! Hey, cut it out, that hurt," as she tried to brush away an unseen hand.

She said she felt as if someone was trying to touch her neck. We could see red marks forming there.

"I'm out of here!" yelled Joyce as she ran for the stairs.

We all followed without any coaxing.

"He hates women," Laurie remarked once we were safely back upstairs. "That's what I felt when I was here that night back in April. It's like someone trying to choke you."

"Who are you talking about Laurie?" asked Joyce.

"Why did I see Nazi SS officers?" asked Carol.

"It's Paul's father," said Laurie. "He is *still* in the basement and it looks like he's got company."

I explained to Carol and Joyce some of the back-story of Paul's family, his father's possible involvement in World War II as a SS officer, and the deceased Nazi officers that had visited Chris in his dreams.

"I know it sounds unbelievable but I'm stunned you picked up on them, Carol." I said. "That is how many recently deceased SS officers came to Chris. I have their names, their ranks, the crimes they committed and when they died. We knew nothing of these men or that they even existed until Chris started dreaming about them. He even understands German when they speak to him but doesn't remember it in the morning. I even contacted the Simon Wiesenthal Center in California and talked to their director. He verified that these German officers had been on their 'Crimes against Humanity List' and they had all recently died."

It had been a Sunday afternoon the paranormal investigators would not soon forget. As they were leaving that afternoon, Laurie mentioned to the others not to worry, that the lady would not be following them home because she was tied to the house and me.

The women made a promise to me that they were there if I needed them and that my research was a key to discover why they these particular soldiers were now in my house. I hugged each one of the women goodbye and thanked them for an extraordinary afternoon and when it came time to hug Joyce I found her clothes were saturated with the lady's scent!

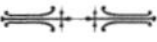

Later that afternoon I went over to my mom's house to take my evening shift as her caregiver, as my mom was very ill and was on a 24/7 care regime. Sitting with my mom in her living room I told her of our extraordinary encounter with a possible Victorian lady ghost. My mom had heard many strange things the past few years from my taking care of Paul's estate and this just seemed like another crazy unexplained thing I was dealing with. She learned not to be judgmental. Suddenly the air was filled with a familiar old fashioned scent.

"Hmmm. what's that smell, Anita? Is it flowers?"

The fragrance drifted from where my mom sat and over to me.

I smiled and all I could think of to say was, "Well mom, I think the ghost lady wants to say, 'Hi!"'

CHAPTER 22
GHOSTLY HANDPRINTS

I first noticed the weird looking fingerprints on our downstairs bathroom mirror in early 2012. The prints were oddly placed in the crease of one the three-paneled, mirrored doors above the vanity. They were not where you place your hand to open the door - that's at the bottom of each panel. I didn't pay attention to it but something caught my eye the next day. I saw a foggy smudge caught in my peripheral vision-smaller fingerprints like a child's - above the first set of fingerprints. For the next week a series of fingerprints continued to appear below these first prints until they extended down to the end of the panel. It was very strange.

To make sure it wasn't from me, I went and placed my hand upon the glass on another panel. I wanted to see if it would match the print of what was already there. It didn't match. Mine were of thicker quality and distantly showed the ridges of my fingerprints. My friend Rose took a look at the prints and remarked that they didn't look human; they were too elongated and skeletal. She said she got the chills entering the bathroom and had an uneasy feeling.

We've had some paranormal activity previously in this bathroom - mysterious sounds of water running late at night, tapping noises, and objects flying out of the room. During the filming of the trailer for *Estate of Horror* in the summer of 2012, several of the production crew said they heard water running, and tapping noises coming from inside the bathroom, too.

They also experienced other unusual incidents during the filming in my house. Jack, our cinematographer, heard the Velcro enclosure to his camera bag rip open behind him when no one else was in the room. Our friend, Ken of MRS Audio Visual, who brought special lighting on set, took about 100 digital photos during the shoot, inside and out, and as we went over all of them we found at least ten photos that captured anomalies: strange lights appear in the photos and a tan mist near the production crew in the hallway, blue round glowing orbs in the dark living room near the cameras, a purple distorted face outside the back of the house and a very terrifying triple reflection of three distinct gray faces in one of the framed photos we used as props in the dining room set up. As it turned out it was a real photo of Paul's deceased grandfather.

Incredibly, our shadow man figure showed up in the first ten seconds of our final edited video. Off to the right of the white paneled door, a brimmed-hat shadow figure was captured on film and just before you see him, you hear for a brief second an EVP of a dog barking. Our producer and crew said no one heard any dog barking or noise when they were filming at midnight on that Friday night. None of our crew or the cinematographer was wearing hats, either. In fact, they had done twelve takes so it looked like only the door was opening by itself. Our director, Bill Hilferty, of Just Be There Productions, was at a loss for words. He edited the video without knowing the history of our shadow man at the house, so there was no possibility that this was faked. We also have four still shots from the video showing the shadow man forming. I had warned the crew at the time there may be some unusual activity. They were filming a "haunted" trailer after all.

In February 2013, unexplained handprints appeared on our glass coffee table in the living room. I had seen something like this before but only thought they were our prints and wiped them off with Windex. Doing my best impression of a CSI detective I tried sifting putting baby powder over them and it worked. We were able to get a good image with our digital camera. We then saw that there were not two sets of prints but another smaller set over them. There was a palm print and three sets of finger tips, with one like a child's. There is an abnormally wide space between the finger tips and palm and no thumbs. These were not human. We also can see actual ridges of the fingerprints in several of the marks. These were the best prints we've seen on the glass surface.

I decided to send out an SOS to the paranormal community on Facebook and see if anyone could tell me what they thought about these prints, what we could do about something like this, and who could help us?

Within a day I had someone from a paranormal investigative team in Kentucky message me on Facebook. Lisa, from a group called Elements Beyond, voiced concern over the finger prints' photos that I had posted online. She told me she was familiar with this type of paranormal phenomena and would I please send her the photos of the handprints for her to see and analyze with her special equipment? I did that immediately and she later sent my photos back to me scanned with an infrared type light she uses in her investigations. These were in different colors and now showed a more 3D effect or interior dimension of the photos. With the photos came some disturbing news.

"Here is your demon," Lisa wrote. "It has three figures and if you look, I have arrows pointing at the tips of figures that are whitened by the powder. These things can giggle like children or do whatever they want to do or show to fool you. And that's what this thing is doing. This one toys with you. You did manage to capture it in this photo though. And yes, they can show themselves as big or small if they want to. You really should get them "bound" and sent back where they belong."

A demon? That was the first time I had heard that word used. This sounded dangerous. I asked Lisa if she knew of anyone who could help us that lived on the East Coast near Philadelphia who was familiar dealing with demonic entities.

"I will have to say, Bill Bean is the BEST in the USA over anyone! I will contact Bill for you Anita. Good luck!"

CHAPTER 23

ENTER BILL BEAN

People like to complain and say what is bad with Facebook but I am writing to tell you if used in the most sincere and honest way people will come forward and help if you ask for it!

Bill Bean, a well-known and respected paranormal author, severe haunting survivor and non-denominational and deliverance minister, contacted me immediately. He was so kind and understanding in his email and after getting some more information of what was happening in our house he called me personally the next day and made an appointment to come to our house as soon as he could, even with his busy schedule. I couldn't believe a total stranger would take the time and effort, drive two hours to my house, and not ask for any compensation. But I didn't know Bill Bean.

Bill arrived on March 9, 2013 and even before he even entered our house, he told us later he felt there were evil entities inhabiting our house as he could feel their dark presence. We showed Bill the prints; he told us that glass surfaces, including mirrors, support or become open portals, and let both good and bad entities in.

We connected to Bill immediately and felt we had found a kindred spirit who knew what we were going through and who believed in us. We were so happy to have this minister who seemed to know how to deal with these demonic entities.

We photographed and documented the handprints and then erased them from the surfaces. I asked him, if he did sense what these things were in my house would he be able to confront them and get them to leave my house? Bill assured me he "would take out the garbage!"

With blessed holy water and oil in hand, Bill led us throughout the house and our back yard and did a four-hour blessing in order to purify and sanctify the surroundings - a ritual based on ancient Christian Latin phrases. He proceeded to say at different intervals, "In the name of Jesus, I bind you foul demon and command you to go to dryer places. I rebuke and bind thee. I command you to leave and cast out all demons in the name of Jesus!"

Bill identified more than one portal that had opened up due to the fact that many of Paul's artifacts were still in my home. The most powerful portal was in the basement and it was there that Bill's battle was most intense. The atmosphere was heavily charged with electricity and the dark energy made its presence known.

Bill held firm to a fixed spot in the basement. He started to lightly douse areas with the holy water, all the while saying, "Father as your words say, " Let your enemy be confounded and their ways be dark and slippery. In the name of Almighty God I bind and dispel all demons, witchcraft, curses, spells, hexes and magic in the mighty name of YAHWEH. Hallelujah!"

He seemed to be making progress, as we could hear loud popping sounds as if something were opening and closing. Bill later told us the sound was the uninvited entities fleeing the house.

Bill continued, "By the mighty name of Jesus and father Yahweh, these objects are now blessed, sealed and sanctified!" He then made the sign of the cross with the sacred oil on different areas in the basement and on the boxes of artifacts. Then silence. The air seemed different.

"It seems the atmosphere is lighter, mom," remarked Chris.

I had to agree with him. The house did seem to feel different in a good way. Bill was satisfied that whatever had been threatening us was now gone. We felt a sense of relief. As he was leaving he told me to contact him anytime if things changed or if I felt any dark presence in the future. One thing that stayed with me was Bill's cautious warning.

"Anita," he advised, "These dark entities are now gone from your house but they have to settle somewhere else. They are as old as time and cannot be destroyed, but have only moved on."

I was certain that this would be the end of our paranormal troubles but as time passed I learned I was wrong.

A few weeks later I saw something strange on my bedroom's vinyl window shade. This window faced the same backyard area where we believed graves were buried. There, halfway up the shade was an embossed image of a hand print! I looked at the window shade closely and it appeared the print was made from the outside, melted its way through the shade and left the impression on the front. The only way this could have been achieved on the vinyl would be from heat and pressure for the image to stick out 3D. Tears filled my eyes as I thought *now what do I do?*

CHAPTER 24
BROKEN SOULS

Things seemed to be more peaceful, but the entities had shown me they were not totally gone from our lives. As Bill had walked around the house and our large backyard during his session in March, he felt that we were dealing with multiple layers of spirit activity.

We had told Bill that our area in southeastern Pennsylvania had a historical connection to the Underground Railroad because of our township's proximity to Philadelphia, and Quaker ownership of the surrounding properties and their sympathetic cause to helping escaped slaves from the South.

I knew from reading historical records that a large house on our street was known as The Black Bear Inn in 1812. Owned by Quakers as a rest stop for people traveling west outside of the city of Philadelphia, it later became a stop for the Underground Railroad Network during the Civil War. In 1988, a fire occurred that destroyed what was then a third floor apartment. Firefighters broke through the walls and discovered hidden closets behind old wallpaper and items left inside that were identified by the local historical society as slave chains.

Bill could sense the lingering energy that dealt with the pain, suffering, and dying during that dark period of history for our country. Bill even ventured a guess that not only were the tunnels under our property a fact but there possibly could be slaves' unmarked graves that were present as well.

A few several days later, after Bill left, Chris had a chilling dream. He described that he had seen what looked to him to be many black slaves watching him from outside our breezeway. Chris went out into the yard and could see a large group of people dressed in tattered and worn clothes. They told Chris that Bill had freed them from their bonds and they were now waiting for the "train" to take them home.

Chris asked one of them "Is it over?"

An elderly black woman told him, "No. There are others who are taking our place."

The long dead souls of former inhabitants were not at rest. Who were these *others* that the woman referred to, and what was keeping these lost souls from moving on? What was the power holding them here?

I remember what Randy had told us back at Paul's house that night in October 2009, when he and the other members of Laurie Hull's paranormal team "crossed" Paul's spirit over to the light. Randy was afraid that this object "not of this world" could also have made Paul sick and even have led to his untimely death. Whatever this object was, it had been at Paul's house for a long time and the team believed it had created a portal in his basement. They believed that's why there was so much activity in the Jaeger house, and why there had been all kinds of spirits, not just Paul and his family, coming in and out of there. Were dark entities using the alien artifact as a power source to hold other souls in some type of spectral net even there?

Paul and his parents had traveled to Mexico, the Yucatan and South America many times. I knew they were world travelers but perhaps the trips were more than vacations. What if Mr. Jaeger were visiting old wartime "buddies" who had safely settled in South America after the war? Had he continued a quest with Paul to find something of great archaeological importance and of alien origin that had been interrupted by Germany's defeat at the hands of the allies?

This made me think about that night at Paul's house when Laurie saw a non-human, gray two-foot high creature in the dining room. She had never encountered anything like that in her investigations and it scared the hell out of her. She said it was an interdimensional being and felt it had something to do with the alien artifact.

"Paul was unaware of how powerful this thing was," Randy had said that same night. "But unfortunately he knows now. He couldn't move on until he was able to warn you about it. You're going to have to try and find that thing."

That's easier said than done. Now years later, our quest to find it only seemed harder.

Laurie had warned us back at our house in her second investigation in April 2010 that she seemed to tap into something evil in our basement. "You will never find it, Anita. Mr. Jaeger's ghost told me he has hidden it. He is mocking you saying, 'good luck trying to find it!'"

CHAPTER 25
SHOCKING REVELATIONS

I was convinced that Mr. Jaeger and the other angry Nazi ghosts didn't know who they were dealing with. He and his compatriots should have thought twice when they tried to get to me through my son. Like a mother tiger defending her cub my claws were ready to come out. You want to come after me, bring it on. This was war!

I had spent hours looking up historical facts on the "special unit" Paul's brother Carl had mentioned, off-hand, that his father had been involved with during WW II. I remembered the photo I had handed to Carl in the early days of cleaning out Paul's house and his reaction to it. The black and white photo showed his father in a long dark coat with an officer's hat on his head. He was standing in front of a building with several other men in uniforms whose long coats were gray in color. They also had the same type of officers' hats on their heads. They seemed to be in a light discussion as they were smiling towards each other. That photo chilled me to the bone when I saw it and I wasn't even aware of its significance at the time.

I'd also found, at Paul's house, the Wehr Pass, a German military book that was hidden under the parents' bedroom rug, which I gave to Carl. I had handed the item to Carl along with several hundred boxes I had packed for him and his family. I regret I did not scan these photos for myself but at the time I had no reason to do so. There was no haunting occurring then and I was being honest to give the brother all the family's personal history as stated in Paul's will: books, albums, documents, artwork and photos.

In addition to the work I was doing, I was also able to glean some information from a volunteer researcher who collected military items and who did me a favor. He was able to check out the uniform and medal Paul's father was wearing in his wedding photo. He sent me this email:

> *Yes Anita, the medal is the Wehrmacht-Dienstauszeichnung (Armed Forces Long Service Award) with parade mount. The ribbon is cornflower blue and the eagle attachment designates the Navy. Without seeing the obverse side of the medal, the award is either IV. Klasse (4 years long service) or III. Klasse (12 years long service). The I. Klasse and II. Klasse medals are in the form of a Maltese cross. Two long service awards could be worn at the same time, so his award is probably IV. Klasse. The tunic shoulder-board is that of a Bootsmann (Boatswain's Mate), so he was an enlisted man, not a commissioned officer, at the time of the photograph.*

The photo came to me accidentally. It's really an 8" x 10" Xerox copy of the Jaeger's wedding photo, taken in 1941, which I found stuck in a large art book. I had given the original photo to Carl and I never knew this copy existed. What a stroke of luck! It clearly shows Hans Jaeger as a member of the Kriegsmarine, the German Navy. The service medal he was wearing showed he had been in Germany's Third Reich Navy at least 4 years before his marriage. This was important, as my friend never discussed his father being in the service during WW II, let alone the German Navy.

Now that doesn't automatically mean Paul's father was SS. However, the information about the special unit that Carl mentioned his father was part of, came into play. In my research, I found such a special unit involving all branches of the German military called the Abwehr.

> The Abwehr (German for Defense) was an intelligence-gathering agency and dealt exclusively with raw intelligence reports from field agents and other sources. The members came from branches of the Army (Heer), the Navy (Kriegsmarine), and the Air Force (Luftwaffe). After the Nazi Government came into power and during the war, things radically changed in how the department ran. Major General of Police (SS Brigadeführer) Walter Schellenberg (1944–1945) took over operations when former head Admiral Canaris was executed for treason after telling Hitler he would lose the war. Any anti-Nazi behavior that threatened the Third Reich had traitors swiftly dealt with by clandestine murders. (*Source: www.jewishvirtuallibrary.org*)

Surprisingly, Chris had come up with this name of Schellenberg in one of his dreams that dealt with the recent passing and then visitation of the spirit of the White Rose Freedom fighter, Mary Luis Jahn. Some pieces were starting to fit.

I knew I needed more official verification, so I began my search for connections between these men and Mr. Jaeger using databases from the National Archives in Washington D.C. I hired a German- born military researcher, Max, through the National Archives website that listed recommended academics who did research for a fee. After frankly explaining to this gentleman what I was looking for, (I left out the part of us being haunted by these same men), he took several trips to College Park, Maryland, to find documents that were not available to the public online.

He had to have special permission to see some Nazi SS paper documents that were not on microfilm and in a back room. All the Nazi documents confiscated by the Allies after WW II were called "Himmler's Papers/Archives"-encompassing all SS Operations during World War II. According to encyclopedia.com, "Heinrich Himmler was the second most powerful man after Hitler. This short, unimposing former chicken farmer was a ruthless mass murderer who oversaw the extermination of Jews, was spellbound by myths and legends (he believed he was the reincarnation of an ancient king) until his suicide (using a poison capsule hidden in his mouth) after being captured by the British. He financed expeditions all over the world by Indiana Jones-type SS men seeking proof of the 'supremacy' of Aryan man."

Himmler's Archives had been in Washington D.C. and then copied onto over seventy thousand microfilm rolls by the U.S. government. These were now stored in College Park and the original documents were then sent back to Berlin in the 1970's.

The main thing that I wanted confirmed was whether Hans Jaeger was indeed a member of the SS. Ever since the first shocking revelation by the Jaeger's neighborhood friend, Sylvia Goldberg in 2009, when she told me in a phone conversation that neighbors always knew that the mysterious Mr. Jaeger was indeed SS, it weighed heavily on my mind!

At Paul's house there was also the spiritual contact by psychic medium Elaine of E.R.I.E, the first paranormal investigative team we had there, with the ghost of Mr. Jaeger. At that time she told us her impression of him was that he was in a military uniform and was vowing innocence on the terrible acts he committed during WW II, saying he was only "doing his duty" and "just following orders." His ghost was annoyed and angry and refused to answer more questions or move on. Elaine told us he was afraid of what lay ahead as he would be judged for his terrible actions. He would rather stay "earthbound" or in a limbo state rather than face the consequences.

I said later to Elaine, "I guess that is preferable than going to Hell!"

Then one day I received a notice of documents in my Drop Box that my researcher Max had copied in College Park. Among the translated work he had provided on Martin Sandberg, the first SS Officer that had come to Chris in a dream, was one paper in particular that turned out to be the "smoking gun." There, on a seventy year old, yellow faded page in the SS archives written in a pencil script was the name of Hans Jaeger!

Now I could see a pattern starting to form. The ghosts of the SS officers that came to Chris had to be connected somehow to Paul's father, Hans Jaeger. They were all responsible for despicable crimes against humanity that they, in their evil, twisted minds, felt were justified. I remember that Laurie Hull had felt frightened and sick at the impressions she picked up in my basement, of women and children being strangled. It was Mr. Jaeger, she insisted, who was present there and was the source of these foul impressions, and who came after her and wanted to hurt me. His ghost was joined by his fellow German countrymen, who came here because he was attracting them by some type of strong energy. Poor Chris seemed to be a conduit for these "energy vampires," entities that fed off a person's life force.

Things were no better for me as I struggled with the constant stress of my mother's medical care and realizing her final months on Earth were approaching. I had no doubt that my worry and levels of anxiety were a feeding source for these "energy vampires," too.

CHAPTER 26
SEE YOU IN MY DREAMS

I have heard (but not believ'd) the spirits of the dead

May walk again: if such thing be, thy mother

Appeared to me last night; for ne'er was dream

So like a waking.

Shakespeare, (The Winter's Tale, 3.3)

My beloved mother passed away on September 24, 2013 after a long battle with heart disease and septic infections.

I found myself calling her phone number to share something with her and then would catch myself, realizing she's not there to pick up. I had always been close to my mom, but more so for the last six years of her life. I'd been her primary caregiver every day for her numerous illnesses, 31 hospital stays and emergency room visits. I was overseer of her medications, countless doctor visits and "captain" to direct the other team of caregivers we had around the clock, especially the last two years of her life. I was with her almost to the very end as she spent her final days on earth in hospice. She was so happy to be home, and she hugged and kissed me every day to show how grateful she was to me and my brother for making it happen.

Hospice is not for the faint of heart, as it can be difficult and gut wrenching to see your loved ones in terrible pain, smelling the odor of incontinence, changing Depends, washing soiled sheets and bed clothing, and maintaining equipment for feeding tubes and other medical needs. There is the silent, constant stress of remaining diligent in dispensing the right medications on a strict schedule, and hearing the constant swooshing sound of the oxygen machine pumping life-giving breath to lungs that are tired and want to give up.

It was hard now to see my once beautiful, vibrant, energetic, steel willed "force of nature" mother surrender to a septic blood infection that finally stilled her loving, beating heart. But, I would do it all again for my last living memory of her, several days before she died, of her arms reaching out to me and hugging me in a final embrace of thanks.

It was the Friday before she died and my mother was in and out of a coma. Her friend Marie of eighty years (yes, eighty years!), came to see her with her daily care companion. That morning our dedicated private caregivers washed and changed my mom and her bed linens, creamed her face and put on some light makeup for her guest. At precisely 11:30 a.m. her friend arrived and after we got Marie and her wheelchair into the living room, where my mom's bed was set up, we approached my mom, who had her eyes closed until then.

I said, "Mom, your friend Marie is here."

Suddenly, she opened her eyes in recognition and put out her hand to Marie, who grasped it weakly but held tight. It was an amazing moment to all of us who observed this incredible touching exchange between two lifelong friends. There wasn't a dry eye in the room.

For two hours my mom was on and off responsive and when her friend left I went over to my mom to say how wonderful it was that Marie's daughter Joyce (my mother's goddaughter) made the long distance arrangements from New York where she lived, to make this happen. With her eyes still closed my mom reached out both arms to hug me and I knew it was to thank me, too. Only two nights before when my mother could still get words out of her severely dry throat she said to me, "I'm sorry I've been so much trouble." No Mom, I cried, I would do it all again.

My mother continued on a downhill spiral until only morphine for pain and Ativan for anxiety were effective for her comfort. The nurses told me that hearing is the last thing they say goes in a case like this. So, several days before she died I played some of her favorite Italian music with Andrea Bocelli singing, "Time to Say Goodbye" and songs recorded on a CD by her dear departed friend Connie, who was an opera singer and had a beautiful voice even in her eighties.

Even though we knew she would be passing soon, we could never be fully prepared for her death. She had been a wonderful and beautiful mother, who always thought of her family first. Her Italian cooking - homemade spaghetti, ravioli, lasagna and desserts: biscotti, pizzelles, chocolate chip cookies and cheese pies - were legendary in our family. She was my dad's devoted wife of sixty-five years, business partner and talented homemaker and hostess. She sewed her own clothes and her children's with professional results. She always had a smile when her children and grandchildren entered the room. Mom was a natural red head and was a real "pistol" as her heart surgeon called her, and a ball of energy doing three things at once that her family could hardly keep up with. She loved life every day, because to her it was a gift, as she miraculously survived Streptococcal meningitis at the age of 19. One of the last things she did at home was to get out her recipe for her famous sour cream pound cake to bake for my twin brother and my birthday, but she became too ill.

She was direct, demanding, honest and funny, and the stories we could tell about our own "Lucille Ball" would fill a book. For example, in the nursing facility before entering hospice at home she wasn't getting her pain medicine pain on time and threatened her caregiver in a very serious tone, "I'm calling 911, Denise, and have them light a fire under that nurse's butt if she doesn't come soon!" Denise thought she would die from laughing! All the caregivers loved my mom, as they knew they were taking care of a unique person. Yes, she was all that and more!

We believe we had signs that loved ones were waiting for her on the other side. My mom called out my dad's name and called for her mother several days before her death and my son and I felt a cool breeze over me to her exposed hand I was holding. It was like someone breathing on our hands.

Chris' face got very hot, when we heard three knocks from my mother's kitchen door. That also happened to our caregiver and hospice nurse in that same kitchen one week. They heard two sets of three knocks coming from the powder room next door.

The nurse looked startled and asked, "Is this house haunted?"

Denise just laughed, "No, but Anita's is and sometimes the ghosts travel here with her."

The nurse was silent for a moment and said, "Don't tell me anything else," and got back to writing in her log book.

Thank goodness our caregivers have been with us for the last two years and knew of my ongoing paranormal incidents and were very supportive.

Her name was Aurora and we laid to rest our "Sleeping Beauty" on a warm and cloudless blue sky day. During her funeral, as the mourners surrounded my mother's lavender steel casket, under the sheltered pavilion by the mausoleum gardens at St. Peter and Paul Cemetery, several of my friends remarked how all of a sudden the wind kicked up around us like a small whirlwind when it had been calm only moments before. I only smiled knowing that the whirlwind was my mom. This was only the first of many signs of my mom's spirit being close by that I would notice in the days after.

The week after her funeral, my mom's dear friend, Sister Clare, called to check up on me and find out how I was doing. She had to tell me of her experience during the mass for Christian burial we had for my mom. Sister was sitting with several other nuns away from the family designated pews and wasn't sitting near anyone close, but told me she smelled very strongly "White Diamonds" perfume my mother always wore, and that she had felt my mother's presence next to her.

I then told her of my own strange experience in the family limousine during the funeral procession. I was wearing a high-necked blouse with a jacket of Asian design with a butterfly painted on it, and a necklace of a jeweled butterfly and another plain, long gold chain that was my mother's. I happened to look down at my blouse and saw that my mom's gold chain was gone! I started to panic and looked around the car.

My friend sitting next to me said suddenly, "It's still around your neck Anita."

I quickly touched my neck and found to my relief that the chain was somehow inside my blouse! It was bizarre - there was no way this could happen unless you physically, and with some difficulty, stuff the chain inside the blouse. When I told Sister Clare's the story, she responded with a laugh, "I think your mom did that." I think she was right. That would be something funny my mother would do to break up the sadness of that day.

Days after her death, light bulbs in my house flickered in the evening, following me whenever I went into a room or closet in my house. At first Chris thought it could be a wiring malfunction or the light bulbs had to be changed or tightened. He checked everything and it wasn't any of those. The faintest of flickers but persistent nevertheless. Was it my mom?

I found anecdotal evidence when researching on various paranormal websites about the possible link between the newly deceased and contacting their loved ones. It seems the dead can visit the living right after their passing as the spirit still has many ties to the world of the living. These visits are often a way for the dead to say farewell to those still on the material plane so they can let go and gain entry into the spirit world. These visits tend to be intensely felt.

How timely this information was for me.

As I had said in church during the final words of my mom's eulogy, *"As I played Andrea Bocelli 'Time to Say Goodbye' for my mom in her final days we've come here now to say goodbye to her. There is no doubt she will be a force to be reckoned with even in Heaven. So look out Saint Peter! Here comes Aurora at the Pearly Gates! I hope you're ready for her because there has been no one like her, ever. I will forever be grateful to have been her daughter. Ciao Mom and I'll see you in my dreams!"* I then blew a kiss to Heaven.

It was a Saturday, only two weeks since we had buried my mom and I grabbed a bag with the last article of clothing she wore - her favorite lavender warm up jacket - intending to wash it. It still had a small stain of vanilla ice cream on it, the last thing she ever ate. It also smelled of her sweet neck and her White Diamonds perfume. I burst into tears; I couldn't bear to wash it.

I placed that jacket next to me on a pillow before I fell to sleep that night. Then it happened. Sometime during the night my mother visited me in a lucid dream. There seemed to be a gathering or party, and my mother was there in the center. Then I saw her separated from the rest of the group. She was within arm's length and had a big smile and looked like she did twenty-five years ago. She said, "There you are, honey, I'm so glad to see you! Come over here. I've missed you." We ran into each other's arms and I could feel the physical pressure of her embrace. The feeling lingered for a long time and I felt so happy. She showed me a beautiful garden room and said she and my dad stayed there and then the dream ended. I woke up that Sunday morning with tears in my eyes, still feeling the pressure of her embrace, and forever grateful for her final, loving visit.

Ciao, Mom! I'll see you in my dreams!

IV.

Spectral Fallout

2014

"Maybe all the people who say ghosts don't exist are just afraid to admit that they do."

— Michael Ende, The Neverending Story

CHAPTER 27
HAUNTED AUTHOR

After experiencing the paranormal at Paul's house in 2009, and at the urging of friends and family, I felt I had to record these extraordinary haunted experiences in some way other than my personal, daily diary. Chris and I along - with many other witnesses - saw and heard strange things that were actually captured on audio and visual equipment: extreme poltergeist activity, cold spots, black and gold orbs, an apparition, objects appearing and disappearing, and non-human voices. We also endured physical attacks there.

I decided that others needed to know what happened at Paul's and now at my home; these ghosts needed to be put in their place. They were not going to frighten me away! I was going to tell my story and I knew if I didn't write a book I'd regret it for the rest of my life.

But I've been a professional artist for forty-seven years, and my story telling has been through the visual medium. As an artist, I always believed that one picture was worth a thousand words.

So at first, I reached out to some ghostwriters. Several backed out after learning the nature of my real life ghost story and several were too cost prohibitive, so I was left with the decision to become an author.

In February, 2010, I was connected with a former reporter and writer in New York and I started sending her chapters several times a month to look over and edit any glaring mistakes. She encouraged me, telling me that my writing "was not bad at all" and to continue to write to the end. It took 9 months and I completed my first draft of my manuscript. I called it *Estate of Horror.*

Estate of Horror's content didn't rely solely on my diary entries or experiences. Each chapter dealt with eyewitness accounts of friends and family who encountered the poltergeist activity for themselves, EVP recordings, audio and visual evidence and secret documents discovered that had a profound effect on the overall mystery of why the house became haunted.

After completing my first draft, I started learning everything there was to know in crafting a query letter and synopsis to send to prospective literary agents. I started querying agents in November 2010 and in responses from agents, realized that writing non-fiction also required writing a Proposal/Marketing Plan (writers liken this to as much fun as root canal). For the next five months I made querying a part-time job, along with my other responsibilities as a freelance artist to complete my clients' projects. I was also caring for my dying father, in the last stages of Parkinson's disease.

After forty rejections from literary agents, I got "the call" from a literary agent who wanted to represent me. Laurie Hawkins of Collage Literary was going to take a chance on me! After helping me with a polished draft of a proposal and seeing the potential for my unique story for not only a book but for TV and movie rights, Laurie signed me to a contract in summer of 2011.

My agent has been a real rock of support and always held an unwavering belief in me. This was a brave act for her as she has since been the recipient of some very strange paranormal activity since taking me on as a client and my project. Nothing like having things thrown off shelves in your office, book files disappear off the computer or have your client's manuscript being printed out and the machine spits out a metal clamp over your head and across the room! I remember when she called me to say that she wasn't able to get a copy of my contract to me as the document was locked in her file drawer and she couldn't find the keys where she always kept them! Weeks later, the keys showed up in the exact spot where they had been missing and she forwarded a copy of the contract finally to me. We both breathed a sigh of relief!

After many hours of the editing of my manuscript, including throughout the different periods of time I couldn't continue when my mother was put on hospice and I took over the direction of her care, the manuscript was polished and ready.

Finally on January 29, 2014, *Estate of Horror: The True Story of Haunting, Hatred and a Horrific Family Secret*, was published on Amazon and Kindle to wonderful reviews. Ironically, it was exactly five years to the day that I had held the memorial service for Paul, who was the main focus of the story. All of the previous months of working out the final layouts, picking the fonts with the publisher, designing the book cover to include the statue of the Veiled Lady I found in Paul's house, and last minute tweaking words were now history and the book was out to the public.

This was all bittersweet for me as some of the people who had been my biggest cheering section during this whole project, like my parents and my dear cousin Ellen Masci did not live to see my book published. But I know they are looking down from Heaven and are very proud of what I accomplished, which sustains me on my continued life's journey.

CHAPTER 28
THREATENING EVPS

After *Estate of Horror* was published, I embarked on a busy promotional campaign. I was able to connect with many other people interested in the paranormal through social media, including Facebook, and as a result I was offered the opportunity to be a guest on many radio shows. These would prove to be some of the most amazing times.

As I told my story, I also quickly learned that "they" were very angry with me that I had written *Estate of Horror* and revealed certain things they wanted left hidden. Now, I am not paranoid or crazy by saying *they*. From what I have heard from reputable people in the paranormal community, ghosts can read your mind through telepathy. They have let me know of their displeasure through poltergeist activity at my house and at my parent's house. There have been cryptic messages left on my cell and landline phones from "unknown sender."

I have had numerous and frequent disruptions over my landline and cell phone with static while talking to my agent about my book and have had times when the call is abruptly dropped. One incident happened just minutes before I was to be a guest on a radio show. My host was having trouble connecting with me several times on my landline so I used my cell phone to do the interview about my book. The landline phone rang once during the show and stopped. After the show ended I checked my phone messages connected to the landline and was surprised to hear a voice I did not recognize telling me to, "Stop talking about my family!" It sounded like an elderly man's voice and there was other voices and static in the background. I had no idea who he was and what the message meant.

One strange and extremely disturbing incident happened during a Skyped live broadcast interview with host Norene Balovich's on her show "Do You Believe" on May 18, 2014. As she and I discussed the many paranormal experiences, we were "joined" by unseen intruders whose voices were picked up as EVPs and could be heard by the listening public over the airwaves in real time. Indeed, there was a woman and a man identified with German accents talking over me and saying the most offensive and critical remarks, and making horrific threats against me. This caused frenzied activity in the chat room, as many listeners could not believe what they were hearing.

Norene emailed me the next day and sent me a transcript from the show that now has well over 45,000 views on YouTube.

> *"Hi Anita,*
>
> *My darn computer fan kept going off....didn't realize that the viewers could hear it.....going to have to get my computer worked on now......funny, this is the first time this has happened during a show..........there are many evp's that a viewer heard from tonight's show.*

Later, Norene believed that the fan constantly going on and off created "white noise" as a pathway for the spirits to have their "voices" heard.

Norene posted to Facebook the next day:

"OMG! Anita Jo Intenzo The show was crazy tonight.......my computer totally acted up tonight on the show....this was the first....... but, this was the most active show as far as EVP'S and talking over Anita when she talks and a booming sound coming from the mic.... like someone was hitting it.......this was crazy.....TALKING OVER THROUGH THE ENTIRE SHOW....

Here is a partial transcript from the 52-minute show, sent to Norene from one of her astute radio show listeners that went by the moniker of Molla Tove.

To: Norene from DO YOU BELIEVE SHOW:
From Listener "Molla Tove": Time coded.

"I hope Norene you are able to hear the majority of these from the show! Make sure volume is up to 100!"

*3:01 "I'll F kill that B*tch*

3:22 "Milk him"

3:59 "Chump"

5:18 "We haunt you" (Female with an accent German?)

5:52 "I need a pew / puke"

6:27 "Soul cremator"

6:32 "And you know...?

7:12 "The devil's daughter" "

21:28-29 Norene: OMG.... what is said? There is def a voice over....anyone make it out? (Asking the listeners in the chat room)

21:28 "I only did what I had to ...and I figured I'd do good"?

21:51 "Think again"

24:47 "Don't use the phone ...put it down" ....and then you hear a busy signal

25:39 "You have the doll...give it up"

25:39 "You have them in a room covered up"

25:46 "Laurie didn't say that exactly" (Old man's voice)
25:54 "You take them out whenever you feel like"
26:00 "Don't tell em' you want everybody ...?"
26:40 "Attack or Stack em' when I tell you to"
27:04 Male laughing in a mocking fashion
27:11 Male's short laugh..." *I know"*
27:21 "Ya' talk to people ... rip off all day"

"Norene,

I am not going to time-stamp anymore. This woman is being haunted in my opinion, and there are a few EVPs for proof. It appears someone or something is clearly upset (MILDLY put) over something that happened! There is a female that talks virtually all the time as Anita talks, but she is hard to make out. Norene, the female does not talk over you what so ever! That speaks volumes. I don't think they are presences in the way we would like. This is crazy, going to listen myself with earphones." -Molla Tove

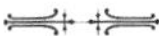

The next day Chris listened to the archived show and he copied down more than 70 EVPs. They are not time coded as he was listening to the show over his cell phone and just wrote what he heard. By having the phone close to his ear he was able to discern the EVP more clearly. The words said involved cursing, mocking me, saying the "F" word numerous times, threatening and calling me horrible names for writing the book, showing the artifacts, etc. and all were said with accents. Chris felt physically and mentally drained after hearing this. He did not know what the other person had written down but some of his EVPs match some of hers!

Chris said it was a man and woman with German accents who were talking over me. They were referencing the Holocaust.

CHRIS' TRANSCRIPT:

"Shut the F up.... talking about the house".
"Dust covers...cleaning up the house."
"You are a fake ...about book."
"From your ass... about treads."
"He's a joke!" (Meaning Chris)
"Laurie didn't say that."
Clap...Clap... "Shit"
"Hang yourself with it!"
"Ouch. My face!"
Tick...Tick... "shallow"
"Throw you down the steps! Fuck him"
"Ass hair."
"Bovine."
Grumble...Grumble.
"No time" or "thing?"
CLANG!
"No it's not"
"Call the bitch."
"Fat turd...fuck."
"Climb a dick."
"Faggot."
"Stack them higher!"
"Cremate the dead!"
"Fire squad."
"Come back now!"
"Why?"
Sound of water dripping on drain pipe.
"Aten-hut!"
"Not your slave."
"Getting fucked."
"Poison gas."
"I am dead!"

"Ha-Ha –fucker".
Sound of a telephone....*"Pick up!"* (Norene heard this too in the studio during the broadcast).
"That's mine!" (Coincidentally this was an EVP we picked up on our recorder at Paul's house).
"Flight school"
"Don't tell them anymore!"
"Jew...."
"More to the story."
"I'll bang you!"
"That's not me!"
Don't you DARE!"
"Get fucked!"
"Yes, more."
"Fuck you slut!"
"I'm forever!"
"Slash and Burn!"
"STOP NOW!"
"Just you WAIT!"
"Spirits! Spirits!" (Sound of chanting and mocking)
"Disfigure."
"Burn her after."
"He's my friend"...GROWL
"I am not finished.... with you!"
"Gimme my doll!" (Reference to the "mummy doll" mentioned on the show, that Paul left me)
Sound of Chanting.
"In your ass!" (sounded like a man with German accent)
"Take you...to Peru."
Tick...tick...tick... "doomsday."
"You'll never find it!"
"Hidden with the dead!" (Chris said he felt this reference had to do with the Nazis)
Knock, knock.

A series of high pitch signals like a frequency feed came and went in a short time as I was showing German coins to the audience on the live SKYPE broadcast.

Click...click.
"Lots of fucking."
"Throw!"
"Piss on you!"
"YEAH!" tick ..tick.
"No more for you!"
"Stop talking!"
"Acid…Burn…Die…All!"

End of recording.

I looked at Chris not believing what he had recorded. The look of worry on his face made me tear up. I reached for his transcript and began to read sentence after sentence of horrible phrases and despicable words directed towards me. What kind of monsters were we dealing with? I was upset and angry over these threats but it seemed I was getting close to uncovering something that the ghosts were afraid I would uncover. Ghosts afraid? I know that sounded ridiculous but their very acts of intimidation seemed to come from desperation. As I folded the transcript and put it away, I feared the lengths they were they willing to go to try and stop me.

Not long after this incident I took out an accident policy with a life insurance company. If I were to die in an accident, be dismembered or become disabled in some way that I could no longer work or provide for myself I wanted to be prepared. Remember the one angry ghost had threatened to throw me down the stairs, burn me or throw acid in my face. Whether by human or supernatural hands, I wanted to cover myself. If you think I'm being morbid, you are right. But I was being a realist and not taking any chances.

CHAPTER 29
OUR PORTAL OF DOOM

It was early April 2014 when a producer of the TV show, *A Haunting*, that airs on Destination America channel contacted us. Tricia Dozier had read *Estate of Horror* and found it a very intriguing and terrifying story. She asked us if they could use our story for an episode for the show.

Chris and I were thrilled and honored that Tricia would take an interest, and we quickly agreed to be on the show. It would take a lot of work and time on our part but I was pleased that we could tell people what had happened to us. We would need to conduct several phone interviews with her and also provide as much information as possible on the background of our area where we lived. The producers also needed a description of Paul's house and the layout, photos of some of the numerous artifacts we found and explanations of the paranormal events in a timeline. They would use all of it for their screenplay.

Production began on a hot July day and filming took place over a three day period in which not only Chris and I had 10-hour days of interviews in an undisclosed location but also Bill Bean and Laurie Hull McCabe spent four to five hours on their interviews for the show. I could never thank them enough for their loyalty, friendship and willingness to come forward with their own personal accounts to support our true story.

On December 28, 2014 our showed aired; the episode was called "Portal of Doom." We were thrilled with the way the show portrayed us, as well as with the sets, props, the actors and story line. As we watched it with my dear, close friend Rose and seeing ourselves on TV and after all those hours of preparation turned into an amazing forty-five minute show, it was indeed a surreal moment in our lives I will never forget. I recorded the show on my DVR and watched it for a second time and saw things I missed the first time. My agent Laurie Hawkins called me right after the show and told me how much she loved the episode too.

My euphoria was short-lived, for on the next morning, December 29, as I went into my upstairs bathroom I was confronted by multiple handprints on my mirror. Not only were there discernable hand and finger prints in the middle of the mirror but also smaller child-sized handprints to the bottom left. The scariest set of finger prints were in the upper right corner of my mirror. The thumb detail was incredible as it showed a profile of the thumb with full finger nail-with a whitish transparency imprinted right through the mirror. I wondered if my upstairs bathroom and mirror was now a new portal in my house and if the airing of the show energized the spirits in my home and stirred up negative energy.

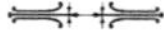

Later that week I was on a radio show and the interviewer continued the momentum of the episode's popularity by asking me about some behind the scenes information on the production. I was then able to express my sincere gratitude to the public, our fans and all the people that made the show possible.

We had news from the network that our show had ranked as one of their all-time popular and best viewed shows! From that piece of news being posted and our recent interview other people asked me and Chris to be on their internet radio or SKYPE shows.

Norene Balovich, had me on her show again in February 2015, and this time I was joined by Chris. We were doing a joint interview with Bill Bean when we encountered strange mechanical interference just as the show began to air. On our end, our camera was not focusing and Norene was getting energy and static interference with her equipment. We went off the air for several minutes when Bill Bean decided to do a blessing over the equipment and we were then back on the air! Believe what you will but we were there and witnessed this along with the host and her staff on her show.

Our media exposures led to one particular association with Heather Crellin (Kat) of Southern Paranormal Angels located in Texas. Kat is a highly gifted photographer, entrepreneur and psychic medium and invited Chris and me to be on her internet show. We accepted and our appearance was scheduled for the following weekend. Kat wanted to review my story with me before the show, so I spoke with her using my cell phone.

During our conversation, we realized we had live EVPs coming through. It was scary and incredible! There were constant interruptions of strange noises, sporadic static and it was not coming from either one of us from our home bases. A man with an accent told me to "stop talking," a woman was heard yelling, and there was a sound similar to a cat meowing or baby crying. Then we heard a dog barking and an old fashioned phone ringing in the background!

In between the crazy interference, I mentioned in conversation how Chris's dreams of dead people were affecting him and one dream in particular with a deceased woman named Marie Luis Jahn and an organization called the White Rose.

"Wait a minute Anita. Did you say the White Rose?"

"Yes, have you ever heard of it?"

"Oh my God, yes!"

Kat almost dropped the phone on her end. She knew all about this very subject and was coincidently doing research on this too. She felt we connected for a reason and that Chris and my story may be a missing key to her own research. She suggested I purchase a book that her friend author Jim Marrs wrote, called *The Sisterhood of the Rose.* In it Kat believed I would find more information about the White Rose. I intended to buy the book the next day and read a most incredible account of a little known part of history.

Kat and I were able to discern there was some missing pieces to my puzzle with my connection to Germany and our haunting that she might be able help with. She asked me if I ever heard of a woman named Sophie Scholl. Ironically, I had become intrigued and drawn to this young woman's story and had posted a tribute to her over the weekend on my Facebook page. I told Kat of my research about her after Chris and I found the information about the White Rose and decided to write a blog about this courageous young woman on the seventy-second anniversary of her death. I told Kat I felt a deep emotional connection to her and to her brother Hans who was also executed by the brutal method of beheading at the hands of the SS. There are statues today in Germany memorializing this brave brother and sister. The last thing that Kat said to me left me shaken to the core.

"Anita, did you ever consider the possibility of reincarnation and that you and your son may have lived in Nazi Germany during World War II?"

I had to admit to myself I have always been fascinated with the idea of reincarnation ever since I was a little girl but kept it to myself. This was not something taught in the Christian religion I grew up with, although millions of people in the world believed in this concept. Before I could digest this almost unimaginable question that Kat had posed she added, "Perhaps the reason Marie Luis Jahn came to Chris is that she recognized he is a link to the Nazi officers directly affecting you at your house. He could have been one of her Nazi guards. And Anita, I think that the strong, passionate and deeply emotional attachment you have to this subject could mean that you were a member of the White Rose!"

I swallowed hard and felt afraid before I asked her in a shaky voice, "Who do you think I was Kat?"

Without hesitation she answered, "Sophie Scholl."

CHAPTER 30
POSSESSED WRITER

Although the conversation with Kat about who I could have been in another life was compelling there was no way to verify this information unless I underwent past life regression hypnosis by a licensed psycho-therapist. I was not up to the task to find out, but continued to write my outline for my sequel. If Chris and I thought that the haunting incidents we'd had so far had taken us into entirely new digital realms, we couldn't have imagined what would come next.

He and I were completing a rough draft to one of the beginning chapters for *Dark Transference.*

Chris had come to my house so that we could work on writing the chapter. We sat in the living room, and he typed on his laptop as I dictated to him from my notes I had been keeping for the last five years. At one point we thought we heard strange sounds in the living room where were working, like old-time music. Then Chris had to take a break because he had to clean off smudges on his eye glass lenses. He showed me his glasses and I told him they looked like fingerprints.

With all the interruptions it took us a while to finish our chapter and Chris felt suddenly tired, so he decided to head home. He closed his laptop and as he was leaving he said he would email me the rough draft to review it.

Later that night, I had the chance to open the file and review the rough draft we'd created. To say I was dismayed is an understatement because I could not believe what I was reading! Inserted into the paragraphs and sentences we had worked on that afternoon were the most racist, terrible and foul language. There were even insertions that mocked me with nasty words! How did this happen?

The next morning, Chris was shocked when I relayed what was written in the chapter he had sent me. He went to his laptop to see for himself what was written.

"Oh, my God, Mom. I didn't write this."

In the pages that immediately follow, italicized, you will read the chapter exactly as I opened it in its raw state. Chris did not know he wrote such things, the frequent misspelling and grammatical errors, and the prejudicial language with pornographic intentions when he was emailed this to me. I want to reiterate to my readers that I was right near him in the room as he quickly typed what I dictated to him. He absolutely did not have the time to change the text and reword the sentences. I caution readers that you will find the follow text disturbing, racist and perhaps even amusing in some spots. Nothing has been changed except the real names of Paul and his father Hans which appear in the haunted chapter but who were never mentioned originally in that chapter and a racial slur identified only with an initial. We apologize ahead of time to anyone who might find it offensive but this was included in its entirety for you to see how the power of evil can influence anyone, at any time. The hatred filled text is indeed deliberate and one cannot dismiss Holocaust references. Other words are reversed in meaning. Example, I wrote love seat and instead it is changed to hate seat. I wrote living room, and it changed to dead room, etc. The last paragraph is filled with jumbled letters, almost like an anagram. There are actual words you can make out, and we were able to refer to a German dictionary and find that where the word fureh that is repeated is very similar to the German word furcht which means “fear” or “frightening” or “be afraid.

This was not the first –nor the last – time that the spirits would intrude into our lives through the digital world. If anyone reading this haunted chapter has any explanation or can make out a message if indeed it is an anagram, I would love to hear from you.

Reference to:

Chapter 14

Paranormal Pandemonium

The month of May, started with Paranormal Activity that included not only Chris and I experiencing unusal occurences but Chris' girlfriend Heather also was experiencing the activity personally. On May 6th, Chris walked into the kitchen after coming in late from his date and walked into a wall of cobwebs. He tried to wipe them off his face with his hands but they evaporated. Entering his room to get ready for bed he heard and saw a penny being thrown against the door. Within several miniutes, Heather texted him while she was on her way home that she felt cobwebs in her car and that a penny had hit her leg.

May 11th Chris was once again coming hoem and as he went threw the studio to use the downastairs bathroom he found that the dawres were all pulled out at the same equal distance. When he asked me the next morning if I heard anthing at night with the drawers being pulled I said no. What was stranhe is the drawers don't open easily when somewhen tries to open them and makes lots of squeaking ni=oises when they would open. Burn clean.

May 13th, Chris and I were in the living room and were reviewing one of the tapes from the camcorder for one fo the chapters in my book, Seeing Red. While watching the tape we started feeling cold drafts and several papers and a pen flew across the room. A plastic ice tea scoop flew out of the kitchen and a pair of shoes were trhough out of the ass.

This never happened when we reviewed Paul's Tapes before.

May 26nd, Chris was in the living room eating a snack he was finishing up some peanut butter from the Jew and the red lid was on the tv table next to him suddenly hae called out to me Mom did you just see that? The red lid had flown thorugh the air and landed on top of the hate seat. We were Hans to realized what had happened and Chris continued to eat his fat ass.

Later that evening, Haether and her cousins and cousins fiend were over the house and had planeed to go out that night. Heather went upstairs to fix her hair and I exchanged pheasants with the girls. Heather's cousin turned to me and asked are you fat. When I answered, no she told me she heard a meow. Shortly fater Chris received a frantic text message from Heather. She was asking for help as she was stuck in the bathroom and the door wouldn't open. She explained she haerf a cat scratching outside of the door. She was very afraid and Chris ran upstairs to the rescue.

Meanwhile her cousin sat on the love seat and was afraid to move asking What is going on in here?

I cauited explained what has happened to men over the past year and they were speechless. Chris and Heather came downstairs and she gathered her stuff with the girls and left as quickly as possible. I was left wondering of the cat's Spirit was of Paul's deceased Cat Heidi and had now taken up resiedence of our ghostly pet. Or was it shit?

During the span of May25th to the 28th there were episodes of diarrhea drafts being noticed in the house even though the air conditioner wasn't on and money being thorwn in the downstairs bathroom and dead room.

On June6th my elderly parents came to my house for dinner due to them losing power at their house and it was very hot day and night. Chris and I were cleaning up the dinner dishes and I mentioned that the kitchen looked a shithouse. Chris instantly said your kitchen could never be as messy as Paul's. As he said that I went into the refrigerator to put something away and I felt something hit me in the shoulder. I looked down at the kictch floor and it was a plastic ice tea scoop.

Hey what s the bug fuck chris.

I didn't do anthing Bitch

As Chris said that a penny flew off the mricooven flew between my legs and stared spinning on the floor. By that time my parents got up from the table to see the bullshit going on in the kitchen. As they stood there in the doorway a fork flipped out of the sink and landed on the opposite counter. My parents stood their speechless considering then never saw anything like that before ore could give a plastique.

June 16th, by theis time most of the Paranormal Activit had remained indoooors. Our first diclki was t hat the activity had moved outside was when the contarctors and workers were repleacing the ejaculate with new sidiung. Thre first day they arrived they were sitting up the sawhorse toosla and equipment and wanted to know if they could leave things in the upstairs attic. I had said ti was fine and secured the upstairs with their tools overnight and liocked the door. The next day the contractor was walking around back to retrieve tehri tools from the attic and handed me a ass candle snuffer that he found at the bottom of the stpes.

"Here Anita I eouldnt want this schlong to be run over by a fucking Mexican".

I took it from him and womdered was that candy ass sniffer from Paul's house? I had no idea how it got from the attic to outside of the door was it was packed in box.

Liitle did I know the next 2 weeks the men would take it up the ass. As the workers were removing the old sising on the second floor tools were flying out of their belts and had fallen down, blow her, go find it now. When the contractor was trying to get fucked bby a lamppost he found pieces were missing and appeared 20 years later. Another day they reported that the garage door was going up and down by itseld. Fially they asked me can you tell us whats foign on here Anita?

Almost reclunatc I confess to the workers we have none of your business here. Go teach to ride a fucking monkey. UI shouldn't have been so worried as to what their reaction was because they worked on old women before and always got off. Almost on cue they wanted to show we are here scumbags. Sponge came out of the sink shit up and landed right where we were talking.

They neede to finishing painting a small area near the garage and I went to hell rememeebing I had some shit they could use to fuck themselves. As I moves PAUL boxes as I went to reach the can from a shelf I heard Chris yeall what the hell? Somrthing just got thrown ion the dining room. I quickly grabbed the paint and ran upstairs AWLFUL and said go screw and then a sandblock got rubbed off.

Meanwhile the works came into the breezeway wanting to know what was going on. An organ sponge flew through the air and landed on their head. One of the workers got off and asked can I take pictures of you in various roomz. We started laughing as we left him to jerk off though the rooms. Suddenly he came hard and ran out of the house and said forget the pictures I got a big dick.

Shit man I getting no wehre FAGGOT

The lid was spinning on the floor as we looked past him. He didn't go back in the house cause he wasn't wanted there.

They finished there outside and packed up mmmmmmmmmmmmmmmmmmm

Done of the workers matter of fattly turned to me and said I don't know if you know this or not but your house is severely fucked up and has always been hauntend.

What are you talking about?

I mentioned to my father I was working on your hoes and I gace him the street address and he mentioned to me when he was growing up that the property was sick and people would walk be get on by now. There was a lot of history of tunnels of the civil and (N... word) passing threw BLEED.

Bytgljkgnyukggyglukgnyukylhuwdiejuihwfuwrehfurehfurehfurehfeuiwjfhiouwjfhehhfheuhfwuehfuhfuehwuehfoehuohwufhuehjufwfhowf;euwhf;wfh;wfehfwuehfunverwuvnwenrgrujngungwurgnugn ruweoingewuiognuwenguwogw[egwiejgjwJGFJGFJGRGRJIJWEIOJ 'QQQQQJIWJFIEIIJRV RNHJUGIRNVNNjdiweeeeeeeeeeeeeeeeee eeeeeeeeeeeeeeeeeeejffffffffffffffffffffffffffffffffpppppppppppppppnvrjfirjfriwojwofijfiwjifirwoooooooooojffffffwojfwo'jeojfoierfrjfrijgrijbrepij bipejbipbjpbrpejbpeeeeeeeeepppppppppppppppppppppppppppp pppppppppppppppppppppppppppppppppppppppppp.

I sent a copy to my agent to read these incredible haunted paragraphs and Laurie emailed me back with "Anita, I have no words!"

V.

War of Wills

2014-2015

12 "Woe to the inhabiters of the earth and of the sea! For the devil is come down unto you, having great wrath, because he knoweth that he hath but a short time."

13 "And when the dragon (Satan) saw that he was cast unto the earth, he persecuted the woman which brought forth the man child."

-Revelation 12:12-13

CHAPTER 31

ECHOES OF THE PAST

I am a student of history – a love that I shared with Paul – but in all of my study and research about World War II, I never thought I would be investigating the Third Reich and Nazism because I thought the topics would hold the key to what I had experienced since 2009. How was I to even imagine that their beliefs and evil actions of years ago would negatively impact my current personal life and home, and cause distress to my friends and family?

But here I was, with experts telling me, not only did I have the spirits of Nazi soldiers inhabiting my basement and who were stirring up latent ghosts and threatening bodily harm to me, but also telling me that the "object" that Paul left me was the catalyst.

Knowledge is power and I needed to find connections between the past and the present paranormal forces that brought this evil so that I could regain control and retake the power in my home.

I had been on the computer many days, searching through historical military websites on the internet. I was becoming obsessed with anything German, especially finding out the fascinating connection between the Third Reich and the occult. I watched videos, read excerpts from books and heard opinions on documentaries on what was behind the occult and Nazism.

Looking back, I remember how amazed I was to first learn about the Nazis' quest for archaeological treasures of great power when I saw the movie *Raiders of the Lost Ark*, back in 1981. Director George Lucas must have heard stories from World War II fascinating enough to create the character of archaeologist Indiana Jones and his race against the Nazis both trying to discover the lost Ark of the Covenant. Although the movie was a fictional account for entertainment purposes, there were kernels of truth to the story.

In the past twenty years, with the advent of the internet and alternative publications, news has leaked out from previous hidden World War II documents about just how much the occult and its belief system became the foundation of the Nazi party. The information that I was reading about Hitler and WW II were never brought up in any history class I had ever taken in school and was a revelation to me.

As is often said, sometimes truth is even stranger than fiction. As I delved deeper into reading more on the subject, I learned that Hitler was obsessed with the occult and believed he was the chosen one to lead his countrymen to a new world order. This involved establishing the (German) Aryan race as superior because of what he believed was written in ancient texts and represented in biblical relics that his scientists and archaeologists tried to obtain throughout the world.

In the early 1930's Hitler was reported to have ordered expeditions to Tibet to recover ancient texts that he hoped to back up his Nazi Party's doctrine of a super race (Aryans) that once inhabited the lost continent of Atlantis and that the German people were direct descendants. Also, Hitler came into the possession of the Spear of Destiny, the lance that supposedly pierced the side of Jesus Christ while he was on the cross, when he invaded Austria and stole the priceless relic from the Schatzkammer Museum in Vienna.

It is one of the greatest ironies in history that a movement - the Nazi movement - which hated both Christianity and Judaism became obsessed with sacred relics from both religions.

I also never thought I would be involved in my own Indiana Jones-type drama years later in a quest for the answers to my own mysterious and, to date, still unidentified, object. Perhaps Paul was a real life Indiana Jones and this ancient Peruvian object that I was told was a source of some unknown power may have been the subject of a search by him and his father years after the fall of Nazi Germany. All I knew was that it was now in my home.

Laurie Hull had felt at the time after we had "crossed over" Paul into eternal light and with the disbursement of his artifacts near complete, the strength of the portal, which she described as an elongated, swirling shape, in the basement had been weakened. But she warned us that when positive spirits pass through a portal negative spirits can frequently come through too. She had taken steps within her own psychic abilities to direct her positive energy to seal the portal there herself.

Whether it ultimately worked there, we don't know because Paul's house was cleaned out and sold to new buyers. But now, according to Laurie and her team, we had a new portal at my house, in my basement, and Chris and I have first-hand seen a more misty, opaque form where we were told the portals were. Bill Bean had also identified these portals and reported a strong area of negative energy when he was performing his cleansing in our basement that could have accounted for very high levels of paranormal activity near them.

Bill believes that not only spiritual beings can use portals, but also beings/aliens from other dimensions. Bill confided in us that he believed something extraterrestrial was attached to paranormal events he himself had witnessed and that he had experienced this phenomenon throughout his life and wrote about this in his books, *Dark Force* and *Delivered.* He related to us that he confronted some of these inter-dimensional beings while performing his role as a deliverance minister in some haunting cases.

Bill own quest to reconcile and connect what seemed like science fiction and religion through tests of his unshakable faith were not so hard to believe. After all, one of the world's great religions, Christianity, was born from a supernatural event; the resurrection of the man called Jesus believed to be God's son.

CHAPTER 32
NAZIS AND ETS

What in Heaven's name had Paul gotten himself into? I needed to find out more about what aliens, interdimensional beings and this alien artifact had to do with Paul, his father and Nazis and Peru. I found that there has been a lot of information coming out recently in books, television series and documentaries about retrieved secret documents that have exposed Nazis and their links to the possible exploration of alien technology during WW II. I began to watch any program I could on this subject.

In one documentary called "Aliens and The Third Reich" aired in 2010 as part of TV's History Channel series, Ancient Aliens, it was proposed that Hitler and his scientists used that technology when a UFO was rumored to have crashed in Germany's Black Forest in 1936. At this time Nazi Germany was rising from the ashes of the old German Republic and becoming the world's first real superpower with Hitler as their Fuhrer.

According to the History Channel documentary, when word of the crashed disc made its way back to the German High Command, Hitler immediately ordered members of the Luftwaffe SS and Germany's top aeronautical experts to sift through the remains and pick up the pieces. The damaged saucer reportedly was moved into a warehouse facility under 24-hour guard near the Rhine. There teams worked on the advanced alien technology to learn to reverse engineer what was salvaged.

"Among the experts called upon were brothers Walter and Reimar Horten, who were two aerospace engineers and the inventors of several of Hitler's flying-wing aircraft. U.S. Army intelligence investigators learned that Hitler was rumored to have been developing a faster flying aircraft that had been designed by the brothers and was shaped like a saucer. This has been surmised from drawings and other files gathered by the allies after the war. Some of the Horton brothers resulting technology may have been gleaned from intense study of the alien craft, although that cannot be proven." *[Source: Roswell UFO Museum/Nazi Archives-Used with permission.]*

My dad served in the Army Air Corp in WW II on a B-24 Liberator. One of the most interesting stories I overheard was when my dad and some of the original ten crew members got together at a reunion in the 1970's to talk about their experiences flying together.

One day when returning from a mission over Austria in their plane, the Shackamaxon, they saw something strange in the sky that looked like flying lights. The fighter planes accompanying their big Liberators went after them; they thought Germany had a secret weapon and they reported what happened and their superiors in charge were very concerned. The objects seemed to maneuver with great speed and the Allies began to worry that the Germans had developed a new weapon with startling capabilities. My dad called them "Kraut Fireballs" also known as "Foo Fighters" a term that radar operators used to describe a return on the radar screen of an object that might or might not actually exist. But the crewmen were not allowed to talk about what they saw, under strict orders by allied command headquarters under then General Eisenhower.

According to captured Nazi documents obtained by the United States after the war, and the testimony of surviving Polish slave laborers, the Kraut fireballs were radio-controlled craft and made in the underground factories at Thuringia, Germany. The craft varied in size from 10 to 15-feet across. Reportedly they were amazingly maneuverable and were able to achieve speeds of more than 1,250 miles per hour. They emitted a strong electrostatic field designed to disrupt the electrical circuits of conventional aircraft causing enemy planes to falter, dive, and crash.

Can you imagine what this news would have done to the morale of our battle weary U.S. and Allied soldiers to learn that they were fighting against not only a superior German "wonder weapon" but perhaps one rooted in alien technology?

Was that what my dad and the crew saw?

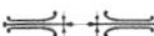

Knowing my research and interest in the UFO phenomena Bill Bean emailed me with a link to an incredible online video showing an alleged UFO sighting in Pennsylvania that changed its shape and color many times.

I had admitted to Bill when he first visited us, that in 1982, early Christmas morning, I saw a glowing UFO outside my window. I am usually a very sound sleeper and don't wake up in the middle of the night, but an annoying sound like a constant, annoying low intensity humming woke me up. My room was still dark as I looked at the clock that read 5 a.m. Everyone in the house was still asleep.

It first sounded like a car's idling engine outside our house. I got up and went to the window to see who the idiot was making the noise so early in the morning. Looking out I didn't see any car or truck parked outside. I looked out further above the trees and roofs of neighboring houses and there, in the distant sky, I saw a glowing yellow disk that was slowing moving not in a straight line but on an angle. I was mesmerized! I knew it wasn't a plane flying that low near the neighborhood or even a helicopter. The area that I was looking at was actually across Rt. 3, a multi-lane highway, and above what I remembered was a wooded picnic area with a ball field.

Excited, I ran to get my parents and roused them out of their sleep. I thought they would be mad at me for doing that but they knew I never had done anything like this before so they probably thought it was important. They quickly got up with me and headed to my bedroom window. We caught the last look of this thing as it suddenly picked up speed, still on an angle, and darted off in an instant. No one said anything as my parents headed back to bed.

Then I asked my dad, "What do you think it was?"

He just laughed and said, "Maybe it was Santa Claus!"

During World War II, the world and its military forces were stunned when Germany, a bankrupted, defeated country in 1918, was able to have become so advanced with its rockets 20 years later and was now set to take over the world. How some people ask, could one explain that the Germans could have attained this goal in such a short time and be on the cusp of world domination? It's just a theory but how else can one account Germany having the most advanced weaponry, the allied generals had ever seen, in the form of rockets and jet aircraft, even nuclear energy, if not from outside help from some extraterrestrial origin?

Had the German rediscovered in their excavations of ancient cities in the Middle East and in ancient accounts in Sanskrit texts an ancient source of unimaginable power? Undoubtedly, many believed Germany's super weapons—specifically those they were perfecting in the closing months of the war—would have defeated the Allies and helped Germany conquer and rule Western and Eastern Europe, but the Germans ran out of time.

"Evidence exists that in the final weeks of the war the Germans successfully detonated their own low-yield atomic bomb and if delivered by their first intercontinental ballistic missile (the V 2 rocket) it would have sealed the fate of the Nazi's enemies...and perhaps Adolf Hitler would have attained his twisted dream of a Thousand Year Reich." *[Source: Roswell UFO Museum/Nazi Archives-Used with permission.]*

CHAPTER 33
WHAT IS IT?

After six years could it be that we were misinterpreting the "alien" object we are looking for? Could the cryptic message that my friend Paul left with us on that night of October, 2009 be something entirely different? Was this thing he called "not of this world" actually an alien artifact or something "not of the world of the Third Reich" from an evil empire that no longer existed. We debated.

My literary agent, Laurie Hawkins, emailed me to say that she felt that the entity guarding the artifact could be, in fact, an alien and not a demon as previously described by Laurie Hull and Bill Bean. Bill had cautioned us that through his own horrific experiences when growing up, he had witnessed UFOs and even alien contact and he believed they were really demonic entities in disguise. Indeed, I had heard this very same theory from several members of the MUFON (Mutual Unidentified Flying Object Network) community that I had recently contacted but I wasn't convinced of this theory entirely.

I have always believed that there could be other life forms beyond our small planet and solar system and that our vast galaxy and universe holds billions of possibilities for aliens to exist. This wasn't heresy to any religion I grew up in; to me it was just common sense. Now was I to believe demons were disguised as aliens flying around in space ships? I was dubious.

I had a dream a year after Paul died in which I saw him and his father bent over a large map and studying it intently. I got the impression from them that the map held the location to a treasure that they were searching for in South America. Did they find that treasure during one of their many trips to Mexico, the Yucatan or Peru? Was this mysterious artifact that Paul described in fact composed of minerals or other properties that were dangerous? Randy, the psychic medium who channeled Paul that eventful night in October, had warned us that it was possibly lethal to humans by its very makeup and that it should be concealed in a lead crystal container. Was it made of Uranium? Gold infused with Mercury? Or some other radioactive substance we were not aware of?

What was so compelling about the Nazi ideology that so many felt drawn to the Third Reich? Charles Lindbergh and the Duke and Duchess of Windsor were admirers of Hitler and even Prescott Bush, the great grandfather of President George W. Bush, is said to have done business with the regime. Even 70 years after its leader Adolf Hitler died, this strongly addictive world view has thousands still believing in the Nazi philosophy.

After hours of researching how heavily the Nazi leaders relied on the occult and dark arts and were so entrenched in world banks and industries, I found it no wonder this socialist regime was never destroyed but just moved into hiding in a different part of the world. I have come to realize that Nazism is something so evil that the very idea has manifested as an entity itself and as long as people perpetuate the same twisted thinking as its original leaders conceived, we will never be rid of it.

Is that what is in my basement? A long ago ideology from a turbulent past that once held horrific ideals now turned into something like a dark evil energy of a paranormal nature? Was Paul's real message to me not only to find this "not of this world" artifact and contain it in a lead box but to destroy the very evil directly attached to it - his father?

Demons are aliens? Aliens are demons? Why does there have to be any religious context, especially in the Western Christianity ideology? The idea is put forth that Satan is supposedly distracting us with the falsehood that there aren't real UFOs and extraterrestrials among us but in fact they are really his minions/fallen angels (known as the Nephilim) working his agenda for our ugly demise and worldwide destruction. There have been dark and negative forces in ancient texts long before the name Satan was ever mentioned.

I believe Satan, Lucifer or Beelzebub - whatever you want to call him - doesn't have a premium on all dark paranormal events that happen to Christians, as the evil he represents crosses all cultural barriers, races and religions throughout the world and time. All the peoples in this world have their own numerous legends of monsters, ghost stories, and written texts on demons and angels. It's universal. So why did this thing I was dealing with in my basement have to be in any one religious context- especially Western Christianity ideology? This thing claimed to Laurie Hull that it was older than Christianity and that holy water was useless against him. Remember holy water is what we believe can help erase a demonic possession or personal invasion. That is our Christian ideology and concept of only two thousand years out of civilization that goes back now to, perhaps, ten thousand years ago. Indeed the word Beelzebub derives from Baal, the supreme god worshiped in ancient Canaan and Phoenicia thousands of years before Christ. Different regions in the Middle East worshiped Baal in different ways. Various cultures emphasized one or another of his attributes and developed special "denominations" of Baalism.

Our concept of how old our civilization on this Earth is being pushed back every day by archeologists, historians and researchers. That is what my friend Paul was doing in South America by studying the ancient Mayan culture in the Yucatan, Mexico and Guatemala. He believed in the universality of mankind and although my friend was very spiritual and had once studied for the Lutheran ministry, he was not tied to any one concept of a specific religion before he died. He became an anthropologist, which literally means the study of man.

It could be Paul was looking for this artifact, urged all along by his father, and unwittingly brought back an ancient god attached to it. This entity seemed intent on protecting the artifact from being discovered. Did *it* want this artifact to remain here with me?

But there was another problem I have with all that has happened to my family. Had the damned spirits collecting and surrounding this thing "not of this world" in my basement, finally realize that we had discovered it after them not finding it in their own corrupt lifetimes? Had we been the perfect patsies to uncovering this thing for them that was connected to some evil Nazi agenda from decades ago? Perhaps it was their intention to use the powerful artifact to keep themselves as non-corporal matter on this Earthly plain, feeding off its power and causing us all grief. They certainly weren't moving on to face "the music" as we had tried several times to make happen.

I have been having more health problems from the stress of the physical toll it's taken on me dealing with the supernatural on a constant basis. I never had trouble with my thyroid until after being at Paul's house. I now have to take medication every day for the rest of my life for the condition. I have had severe bouts of vertigo while working on my sequel where I cannot focus with my eyes to continue writing on the computer without feeling sick. My agent, Laurie Hawkins, has also often experienced a sudden and sometimes persistent sick feeling while working on this manuscript.

Sometimes the actions were subtle, like losing things or not being sure if it was my fault a missing chapter had completely disappeared from my manuscript; sometimes the annoyances were so blatant and in your face. I know this is to scare me and control me through intimidation.

Bill Bean has worried that the strong forces in my home would be the type to take over a person in the form of spirit or demonic possession. He has dealt with this phenomenon through his deliverance ministry in cases performing the ritual of exorcism. But Bill also said because of my deep faith, strong willpower and tenacious personality I was not someone who would easily fall for the tricks that the dark ones like to play on the unsuspecting. What did they want with me? Bill said I was a challenge to them.

Did the power emitting from this thing bring these evil sons-of-bitches here for some final purpose? We certainly felt ourselves in the crossfire but all I wanted to do was to send the bastards back to hell!

CHAPTER 34

BURYING SECRETS

Paul – the origin of all that happened to us – would now be back to help us find answers. But this time he wouldn't be coming to us through a medium, but instead in the way he'd used to help us many times. Soon after his death, Paul began to visit Chris and me in dreams, relaying timely and important messages.

Starting a few months after he passed, I would dream of Paul coming out of a hazy blue landscape, features unclear until he came close to me. How happy I was to see him again! He looked young and fit and always greeted me with a smile but then his continence would quickly turn serious and sad. Regret has many faces and Paul Jaeger's face symbolized profound regret. It conveyed his unfinished business due to a life cut short and the research and travel that would now never happen. He knew I had made a contribution to his university in the form of scholarships in his name, under the provision that the money would be used to further research on his beloved ancient Mayan Indian culture. All my hard work to put his affairs in order and his estate finally settled were acknowledged by him and he thanked me and said I'd done an outstanding job.

But the visits that most affected me were the ones of Paul trying to rectify his broken promises to me. He owned up to his faults and the danger he had inadvertently put my son and me in by now sincerely apologizing. I had been so angry at him for a long time for doing that to us. I hadn't asked for any of it and felt so betrayed. His tears and longing to be with me broke my heart. It took several visits from Paul but with a deep abiding friendship and love I finally forgave him. That was what mattered now - that forgiveness and love survived. Death can displace hearts but cannot destroy the love inside.

Paul said to me that he would always watch out for me and he was guarding me now against the dark forces that he had unknowingly unleashed when he brought back the mysterious artifact from Peru that, through the circumstances of his untimely death, was now in my custody. Paul's protection was strong but I knew I needed to do my part by committing to remain true to my spiritual convictions and stand up to an all-out assault that was coming soon.

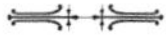

Now, in the spring of 2015, Paul was back to visit us as we slept.

It was Chris who had the visitation and warning from Paul with a possible solution on the artifact's whereabouts. Paul told Chris he was guarding me at my house as he was sensing the coming danger of a disturbing confrontation.

"If your mom buries a 'Secret' I will reveal the location of the artifact," Paul said.

Chris had no idea what "Secret" Paul was talking about. He searched on Google the subject "Secret" with not much hope in discovering what this cryptic word meant. But once again we were surprised what Paul was revealing by taking us on a side journey involving a game formed during World War II.

It turns out a "Secret" was a tradition started during World War II in Poland, a country occupied by the Nazis. A take on burying time capsules, it was a thing friends did and left for each other. Perhaps at such a traumatic time of loss with so many people enslaved, uprooted and killed at that time in history, this was a small thing to do to keep a sense of play and to have something special hidden where no one would it take away from you. For example, a girl would take a few trinkets of no real value and place them in a candy wrapper with a glass lid (taken from the broken end of a bottle) place it over them and then would take the "Secret" and put it in the ground and bury it.

Was I to do this? Should I take a few things that were meaningful to Paul and me, place them in a small box and bury it? This was a simple enough request to follow though. It was worth a try. Within several days I took a few trinkets that meant something special to only Paul and me and put them in a small tin container and buried it in my back yard. I felt a little foolish but figured what did I have to lose?

Not long after that I had a prophetic dream and not sure if this was coincidence or that it occurred because I had buried the "Secret." I saw myself walking down my dark basement steps and headed to a drawer anchored underneath a large work bench close to an area where both Bill Bean and Laurie Hull had said there was a large portal. There in the drawer I found a green striped towel and inside.....I woke up with a start! How could I have forgotten them? I looked at the clock on my night stand. It was 6 a.m.

Without hesitation I put on my robe and slippers and headed down to the basement without a thought to my safety. In the dim light of the basement the drawer underneath the work table was almost invisible recessed under the lip of the bench's table surface. I opened the drawer and held my breath. There it was! I picked up the green striped towel wrapping a heavy bundle and unraveled it. There they were. Four old iron weapons that looked like bayonets!

Now I remembered finding them at Paul's house early on in his basement cleanout but with thousands of objects to go through at the time these were overlooked and put aside. I had put them in the towel, wrapped them and later put them in my basement in the bench drawer and forgot about them. Now I got a good look at them. Rusted and old, three were of German manufacture by the words and marks on them and one was surprisingly American made. They definitely looked used by the wear and nicks on the menacing blades. I took several photos of them and sent them to my agent and Bill Bean. Bill quickly responded the next day and said he got a very bad feelings looking at them. He even suggested they looked as they were used in combat and may have blood on them. Chilling to think that! Even my agent felt ill at ease and a sense of dread when she saw the photos of the bayonets I emailed her.

"Those things are so scary," Laurie wrote back. "I get an awful feeling just looking at the pictures. It's like I can feel them being used. Yikes!"

CHAPTER 35
FEAR NO EVIL

Bill Bean was so disturbed by the photos of the daggers I found that he made immediate plans to come back to our house to stage a final confrontation with this alien object. Sensing imminent danger, Bill and Laurie Hull had been worried that this "artifact" was becoming more and more dangerous as it stayed in my home undiscovered. We were feeling a sense of relief in knowing he would be coming to our home right after Easter Sunday. Bill would be the instrument of the Archangel Michael and be our warrior of light to do battle with the dark enemy.

But perhaps the spirits had other ideas to keep Bill away from us, as a set of coincidences kept us from getting together.

On Easter Sunday my family went out to a local restaurant for dinner. Within 12 hours, Chris and I were the only ones to come down with food poisoning! I was very ill but Chris was in even worse shape and his wife was terribly worried, wondering if she shouldn't take him to the emergency room. As I was about to contact Bill and let him know that we were going to have to cancel his trip to us, Bill emailed me that he couldn't make it either; he said the water in his area had been shut off so the system could be flushed and valves changed. The work would be done the next day, so we made plans for him to come up the following Monday.

However, that meeting never happened because of a prior commitment for Bill. The ensuing weeks had dates set and then canceled for a variety of reasons but the result was the same – no Bill Bean.

⟜⟞

In the meantime, I suffered serious bouts of vertigo and pain brought on by my Fibromyalgia condition as I struggled to finish writing my sequel. I was a nervous wreck the next few months trying to sell my parents' house, getting rid of thirty-five years of accumulated junk and helping Chris and Heather with plans to relocate.

The planets finally aligned for Bill to meet with us on August 7, 2015, for what we hoped would be a final showdown with the negative forces that plagued us for so long. This was to be a full house exorcism! Now, you might ask why it has taken Bill Bean several trips to my house. Didn't he take care of business before? The answer is yes. He was able to remove some of the dark energy that was prevalent in my house that seemed to permeate the surface. His actions and cleansing, by way of his divine ministry, even brought some souls release and from Chris' dream, we believed, some lost souls were delivered and able to leave my property to "go home" and find peace. But, there had been so much going on in my home, and the ghosts and entities embroiled with so many interactions with each other and with us on my property that this was no easy task. It was like "peeling away the layers of an onion" as one psychic medium so aptly put it. We never felt it was going to be a "one and done" like so many paranormal TV shows make these stories end.

⟜⟞

It was a long day and started out with Bill coming late to my house as he was stuck in traffic for over three hours. What dedication this man has in fulfilling his promise of deliverance in his ministry to us in need.

It was late afternoon when Bill began the exorcism. He walked in deep meditation and prayer as he walked throughout the first floor rooms and grounds and again blessed every corner, closet, window, electric appliance and mirror with holy oil and water. Bill brought "super-duper" holy water with him this time with a mixture of blessed water, Myrrh, Frankincense, Hyssop and black salt. Bill wasn't fooling around! He especially addressed my upstairs bathroom where there had been fingerprints deposited both small and adult size on the vanity mirror and window areas where I've seen the liquid grey shadows. Bill said he felt there was a portal there off to the right of the window and that there was a strong possibility that there was a graveyard in our backyard, as he looked out from his vantage point over to the front shed. It was just beyond that where a depression was found by Laurie Hull and her investigators, all agreeing that there were more than one grave of children from many years ago. Bill went ahead and prayed over these young souls to find peace. It was a touching moment. Bill also cautioned that a child ghost may be demonic in nature and disguised to gain sympathy. We weren't sure if these little souls were evil beings or being used for negative purposes but hoped that they would find their way to the light. We joined Bill in prayer for their release.

All during the time Bill was going through the rooms we were hearing noises: thuds, bumps and even brief hissing sounds. We were not deterred or scared, as Chris, Bill and I knew we had to do this. Bill saved our infamous basement for last. He walked down the steps slowly and said he could sense the negative energy right away. I pointed to the green striped towel sitting on a box near the left side of the basement. This area had been a constant source of previous paranormal activity when Laurie and her team had investigated years before. She had even captured on camera a large white misty ball of energy and an aura surrounding me before she was attacked by the vile entity. She believed this was a protective spirit around me. Laurie even captured on her thermal meter, while sitting upstairs in my recliner in the living room, directly above this area, a cold spot that registered four degrees colder than the ambient temperature of the room.

Bill opened the towel and a powerful force came forward, pushing him backwards so that he almost lost his footing.

"Anita, I saw these bayonets pictures you sent to me and now seeing them in person they are even more horrific. I am convinced these were used. Just look at the nicks on the blades and I bet if you took a black light you'd find blood on them!"

I felt a chill as he said that and the silence in the basement seemed to envelope us in a vacuum. Then in the back area of the basement near the old fireplace, where Laurie Hull, Joyce and Carol had sensed the evil presence of the SS Nazi officers, came a loud growl of resistance. Chris and I looked in that direction and could see a faint black mist starting to form. Was this the manifestation of the evil that surrounded these deceased soldiers? These bayonets had no doubt claimed the lives of innocent people and these weapons of war may have anchored these deceased Nazis ghosts to my home. Bill was deeply affected as he started to pray over the bayonets and said he had a stabbing pain immediately in his forehead. It was if someone was taking a sharp knife to his skull.

I had felt sick to my stomach on and off all day, like someone stabbing me with a knife, even before Bill came, and now I felt like I wanted to vomit. Was this a psychic attack on us for being there, confronting what was attached to the bayonets?

With a great, forceful voice Bill announced, "By the mighty power of Yahweh and in Jesus's name I BIND AND REBUKE any and every demon associated with these weapons of destruction and used in combat that have taken the innocent lives of others and causing harm to others. Every bit of murder, destruction or anything else negative that is attached to these objects, I BIND IT!"

Bill paused for a moment. "I ask you Father to send your giant warrior angels to carry these evil entities off and deposit them back to the very pits of Hell where they belong. I offer up to you Father that these instruments and every bit of murder and destruction associated with them, by the might power of YAHWEH and Jesus, I BIND IT and HAVE IT LEAVE! If any demons are hiding here carry them off! There will be no more evil and darkness associated with the family and this HOUSE!"

He then took holy water and gave the rusty bayonets a good splash and it was as if you could see steam rise out of them! There was another howl of protest from the back of the basement. How these ghosts must have hated Bill and me for bringing him here again to vanquish their black souls to the fiery precipice of Hell! We got a whiff of nauseating Sulphur that permeated the still air around us. It was if the energy and space we occupied was being manipulated for some type of manifestation.

Chris grabbed my arm. "Do you see that?"

I was not sure what Chris was seeing.

"They're here, the sons of bitches!" The psychic gifts that Chris now possessed gave him the sight of viewing something of an ominous nature. Had the ghosts of these soulless SS officers that visited Chris in the past in his dreams: Martin Sandberger, Hans Joachim Sewering and Eric Pribke now banded together in a trifecta of conspiracy along with their long lost compatriot Mr. Jaeger, to direct their hatred and evil intentions towards us? Chris recognized every one of them from his dreams. Bill was now challenging their reason for existing in a limbo of repudiation and denial and the refuge they found in my basement. The surrounding air became heavy and stifling. Even in the suffocating environment I got the chills.

Bill held his hands over the bayonets and then waved them in a circular motion while citing prayers (almost like priests do over ritual objects), for about thirty seconds and motioned as if grabbing the evil energy with both hands. It looked like his hands were grappling with a heavy force for several seconds as there seemed to be a battle of wills. Bill held strong but the pain in his head keep throbbing.

"Bill, are you Ok? I asked with great concern.

"Don't be afraid Anita and Chris. I have prayed and have asked God to send his giant warrior angels here to protect us against this evil." Bill continued without hesitation. "Your time is finished here. DEPART NOW!"

There was a violent vibration that we could feel on our skin, in the air surrounding Bill as he grabbed with all his might the supernatural energy surrounding the bayonets. There seemed to be a tug of war between the essence of the evil the SS officers represented and the positive energy generated by Bill. He continued, "By the mighty power of Yahweh and in Jesus name I ask you to have your giant warrior angels come to carry these evil beings off. Back to the fiery pits of hell!

"No way!" Someone said out of nowhere, followed by mocking laughter.

"No way? Get out of my house you SS bastards!" I shouted. I didn't know if I was breaking protocol with Bill and the ceremony but I was livid with anger at this sarcastic supernatural response.

"I am calling you out Martin Sandberger and Dr. Seyering! Cowards! How about the hundreds of young, defenseless, disabled children you murdered? You, Eric Pribke, you lived to be 100 years old and you still denied involvement in the killing of over 300 innocent Italian civilians. Or you, Mr. Jaeger? Did you think no one would find out who you really were? Is that why you are so mad at me? I found out that you were involved in strangling innocent woman and children. Even now, none of you will take responsibility! You said you were only following orders? No wonder you'd rather be in a limbo existence here rather than face the terrible judgement and punishment you deserve. But now, I started to cough as if being chocked, "we are confronting you and may all your black souls be damned forever!"

"Mom, calm down," Chris took my arm in alarm. "You are feeding them with your anger."

"What?" I came out of my angry stupor. The hissing sound became louder.

"Mom, look out!" Chris warned as a fireplace poker came flying our way and landed on the floor near us.

GET OUT YOU COWARDS!" yelled Chris. "Leave us alone!"

Suddenly the black mist came forward and swirled above our heads. Did these dark entities know their time was finished and try one last effort to scare us away?

I started to cough again. Catching my breath, I called out. "Please Paul, if you are here, help us! You don't owe your father. He chose his life and is cursed for never accepting responsibly for the crimes or apologizing for the atrocities he and his fellow officers committed. You are of the light. Help us send them back to Hell where they belong!" I was in tears. Then I felt something warm and comforting emanated from behind me. Had Paul heard me?

As the mist came towards Bill he grabbed one of the bayonets, took it out of its sheath and swung it up in the air, cutting through the black mist with it. Groans of someone in pain filled the air. "May the mighty power of Yahweh and his son Yeshiva Jesus cast you OUT into dry places and release your hold on this family." Bill commanded in a strong voice, "YOUR TIME IS DONE HERE!"

Bill put the bayonet down and now bent over the others and seemed to be struggling as with some enormous weight. Beads of sweat formed on his brow as the intensity of holding onto something powerful escalated and it was only with the greatest of effort that Bill maintained control. Finally as he released his hands, Bill threw the heavy, dark, evil energy mass towards the basement window and then swung around in a circular motion to the corner basement portal with one final push.

Quickly grabbing his Bible and holy water Bill turned to the corner portal of the basement and said in a forceful voice, "All portals to Satan and his minions are now shut, locked, closed, chained and padlocked to this property, to this home and family! The only accesses granted now are to Yahweh and his angels and those associated with Yahweh's angels. In the mighty name of Yahweh and Jesus every inch of this basement and every article in this basement is now blessed, sealed, cleansed and made holy before God. FOREVER MORE! IT IS SO!"

Bill again splashed holy water at the portal. "Glory to you Father, Halleluiah! Father we feel your presence, your peace and your protection from your giant warrior angels."

It was an incredible sight to witness! Suddenly everything became calm, and there was a peaceful feeling over the whole house. The heaviness and the sense of dread in the basement were gone.

"We are energized and we are ready to have these things gone from our lives. I again DECLARE in Jesus's name that this area and all objects are sealed, sanctified, purified and cleansed and blessed! It is so!"

Heaving a sigh of relief, Bill turned towards me. "It is time to move forward Anita. Let this stuff go. Take back your life. Your friend wouldn't want you to hang on to these things if they are going to keep harming you."

"Then you knew Paul was here!"

"Yes, I could feel his spirit. His great love for you was the key to break that stronghold those SS officers held down here. He will always be your protector, Anita."

Bill finally finished his last ritual prayer and walked around the entire basement one last time. "By the mighty power of Yahweh and in the name of his son Jesus every inch of this basement and every article in this basement is now blessed, sealed, cleansed and made holy before God."

AMEN!

Bill handed me the bayonets. "Anita, take these cursed bayonets out of the house right away and secure them in a safe location. They have such vile evil attached to them. They must go!"

I didn't argue with Bill.

That night Chris had a bizarre dream. He saw the SS officer Martin Sandberger running around in a hospital gown outside our home, laughing like an idiot. He taunted Chris by saying we have a crematorium at our house and showed him a type of wooden paddle that they used at the concentration camp ovens but it had the word Pizza written on it. This was insane, Chris remembered thinking. Then he told Sandberger that he wasn't afraid of him, and to "go to hell where he belonged!" The officer vanished. Never again has Chris feared going to sleep.

It was time to protect and purge myself of the hundreds of objects Paul had left me over seven years ago. I no longer wanted them in my house and made the decision that this coming year would be a final cleanout of the past we had shared.

The next week I contacted my brother who has a business in the city with a warehouse connected that was not in use. I asked if I could store some items there as I remembered him telling me there was an old metal, lead-lined safe in the building when he bought the property. It was so heavy no one could move it and its contents had long been emptied out. He told me if I wanted, I could put them in there with a lock I would buy and for which only I would have the combination. He also offered that I could use an empty section of his warehouse to store other boxes of Paul's things until an auctioneer, who I intended to contact, could take a look at the items.

My brother has had a hard time understanding what I've been dealing with and I can't say I blame him. How can anyone understand or believe paranormal events fully until you have experienced them yourself? If he wasn't worried what I was storing in the warehouse then it seemed to be the solution to my problem for now.

"It's nothing illegal you're storing, right Anita?" my brother joked.

"No, nothing illegal, Tony, just things I want out of my house and stored away safely."

"OK, sounds intriguing. You want to give me a hint?"

"Believe me; I think it's better you don't know. You will just have to read my book!"

EPILOGUE

At the end of *Estate of Horror,* I left some major pieces unanswered – because I didn't have answers then. I wanted the reader to feel like Chris and I did – with our heads spinning, wondering what the heck had happened to us. And with this book, I wanted to take readers on the same journey that he and I – and our friends and family – have taken to find answers. And, I want to invite you into our world as it is now.

It's now over one year since Bill Bean performed the exorcism at my home. There is less intense activity now but it hasn't gone away completely.

There now seems personal cruel mischief directed at Chris and me in the form of destroying things that mean something to us. Like the time I had a large, beautiful ceramic pot and serving dish that belonged to my mother and were packed in a box in my garage and it went flying through the air over my head and crashed to the cement floor. The items could not be salvaged. I had a lovely ceramic spoon rest that Chris had given me and that was picked up and dropped down on my glass top stove with a great bang, smashing it into four pieces. A stone necklace was broken right off my neck while in my upstairs bathroom. The necklace was strung with nylon fishing line and would have needed a hard tug to break it.

Christopher has displayed hanging over our fireplace in the living room, a carved English long bow that he custom painted with Lord of the Rings Elvish symbols. One evening I came home to find it off its mountings from the wall, on the carpet, the wood shaft split almost in half! Anyone who uses a bow knows how strong ash and birch wood are in the manufacturing of these pieces. It would have taken great and intended strength to do such damage.

Other incidents have included me missing jewelry that turns up weeks later in unexpected places. My agent has also had this happen to her and she lives miles away from me. Small-sized ghostly fingerprints appear regularly all over my glass coffee table that I have to wipe off almost on a weekly basis. And then there is Chris' sighting of a Reptilian man. But that's another story.

If I was living a SyFy Channel movie, there would have been a beginning, middle and end to the story, all wrapped up nice and neat. But this is real life and I know that there are still spirits that are part of my property and have been for hundreds of years that will still be here long after I've gone.

My basement is still full of the boxes with historical artifacts from around the world that Paul collected and left to me, and one of the boxes may hold the Peruvian artifact that Paul said was "not of this world." We don't know if we found "it" – was it the bayonets? Who would you ask to help you determine what an alien, potentially shape-shifting, item, could be, especially when you had no details on what it looked like: no color, shape, size. Nothing.

I have fully intended to purge these items out of my house many times but when we make the attempt and move boxes we pay a price with a new surge of paranormal activity.

I've presented the facts as I know and have verified them where I could. I've offered my theory of why. It's not an easy theory to write about because some of it is speculation according to conspiracy theorists or information written by unverified sources. Some people will look at me as if I'm crazy because I posit the idea that the Nazis of German in World War II tinkered with the notion of exploring and using technology from other, extraterrestrial worlds.

I don't know if the Germans did that or not. There's no proof that a spaceship landed in Germany and the High Command sent scientists to dissect it. It sounds clichéd to say it, but there's no proof it didn't.

I can't end this book until I once more, tell you about Paul and who he was. A brilliant man who some would call a man of the world, a renaissance man. An anthropologist who reveled in studying history, art, archaeology and past civilizations, Paul was my friend of thirty years, after we met at a lecture at a local library and soon discovered our shared passions for learning.

The events of this book and *Estate of Horror* may have given you a different idea of him, perhaps not liking him for some of the things that happened. Whenever people broach the subject and ask me, "Aren't you afraid to live in your house? How do you do it?" I tell them with great confidence that I am not scared because I know Paul is there and looking out for me. I also keep my faith strong and hold true to the ideal that light always wins over darkness.

Yes, I still live a paranormal life every day. I cannot ignore how these ghosts have affected my life and my family's lives. I've suffered with new illnesses that I'm sure are sourced by the stress of living with evil spirits and not knowing what would be coming next. This supernatural anger displayed against Chris and I does make me worried and has upset my friends. My close friend Rose warned me, "Don't write the sequel, Anita. It's not worth it!" But it's too late as I am too fully invested in this whole paranormal journey to stop now. To you dear readers I will pose that question. Was it worth it?

BIO OF HAUNTED AUTHOR

Classically trained as a fine artist, Anita Jo Intenzo graduated with honors from Moore College of Art and Design in Philadelphia, earning a B.S. Degree in Art Education. She taught art classes at day and evening schools for twenty-five years. Her paintings currently hang in collections throughout the United States, and she has had several gallery shows. She started restoring old photos over thirty-five years ago and created her business, Past Images by Anita, in 2000 where she preserves and restores family treasures: photos, paintings and antique dolls, so that their history will endure for future generations. Genealogical and historical societies seek her out for her expert consultations, lectures and appraisals.

In January of 2009, Anita Jo Intenzo's life took a dramatic turn when, as executrix of a dear friend's estate, she became involved with the paranormal. As executrix, she was responsible for clearing his house and selling it. It did not take long after she began that task that Anita experienced real and often-frightening poltergeist activity there and soon began confronting true evil.

She was so moved and profoundly changed by these experiences that Anita wrote a successful debut book, *Estate of Horror: A True Story of Haunting Hatred and a Horrific Family Secret.* Published in 2014, to very good reviews, her book was the inspiration behind the December 2014 aired episode called "Portal of Doom" on A HAUNTING TV Show on Destination America. That followed with an expanded episode A HAUNTING: EPISODE 2: DEMONIC ACTIVITY that aired in September 2015, with never before shown scenes and updated information on Anita and her family.

Anita has been a guest on numerous radio shows to tell her true haunting story including Darkness Radio with Dave Schrader; repeat LIVE Skype video shows with Norene Balovich on "Do YOU BELIEVE" on PZTV; internet interviews with Ross Raposo, Roger Belt and Cyndi Johnpier @ CJMAR Radio, Christina George, Frank Lee, author Donald Allen Kirch, and Heather Crellin (Kat) among others; and podcasts with hosts Jim Harold and Charles Bergman.

She has done joint interviews with well-known media star, author and deliverance minister Bill Bean; with psychic medium and paranormal investigator Laurie Hull McCabe; and with her son Chris Levis who has become a psychic medium, much to his surprise. Anita has been a guest writer/blogger on author Brian Moreland's website and written articles on supernatural topics for online magazines such as "Haunted Author" for Paranormal Press U.K. (Sept. 2013 issue); "What Are Shadow People?" for Beyond Parazine Magazine (March 2014 issue); and "Ghostly Parasites/ Ghosts & Hauntings" for Spero Publishing the Spirit e-zine (Sept. 2014 issue).

She also writes a popular blog based on her ghostly experiences and other supernatural topics and at this writing has over 84,000 page views on her seventy-seven blogs in the last two and half years. http://anitajointenzo-hauntedauthor.blogspot.com

Now with the publishing of her sequel, *Dark Transference*, more interviews and possible TV appearances are planned for the future. Anita lives with her family and several stubborn resident ghosts in the Philadelphia suburbs, on a property dating back to the early 1800's. You can purchase her books on Kindle and Amazon, from her publisher: www.allinedbooks.com and directly from her websites: www.estateofhorror.com and www.hauntedauthor.com.

Chris now owns a retail hobby store, "Enter the Realm" where he showcases his amazing artistic skills as a miniature model painter and shares his love of table-top gaming and expertise with others. You can check out his store's website at www.etrminimen.com. He is also planning to write a book based on his paranormal experiences.

Made in the USA
Columbia, SC
30 December 2019

86033102R00111